Teacher's Resource Book

3

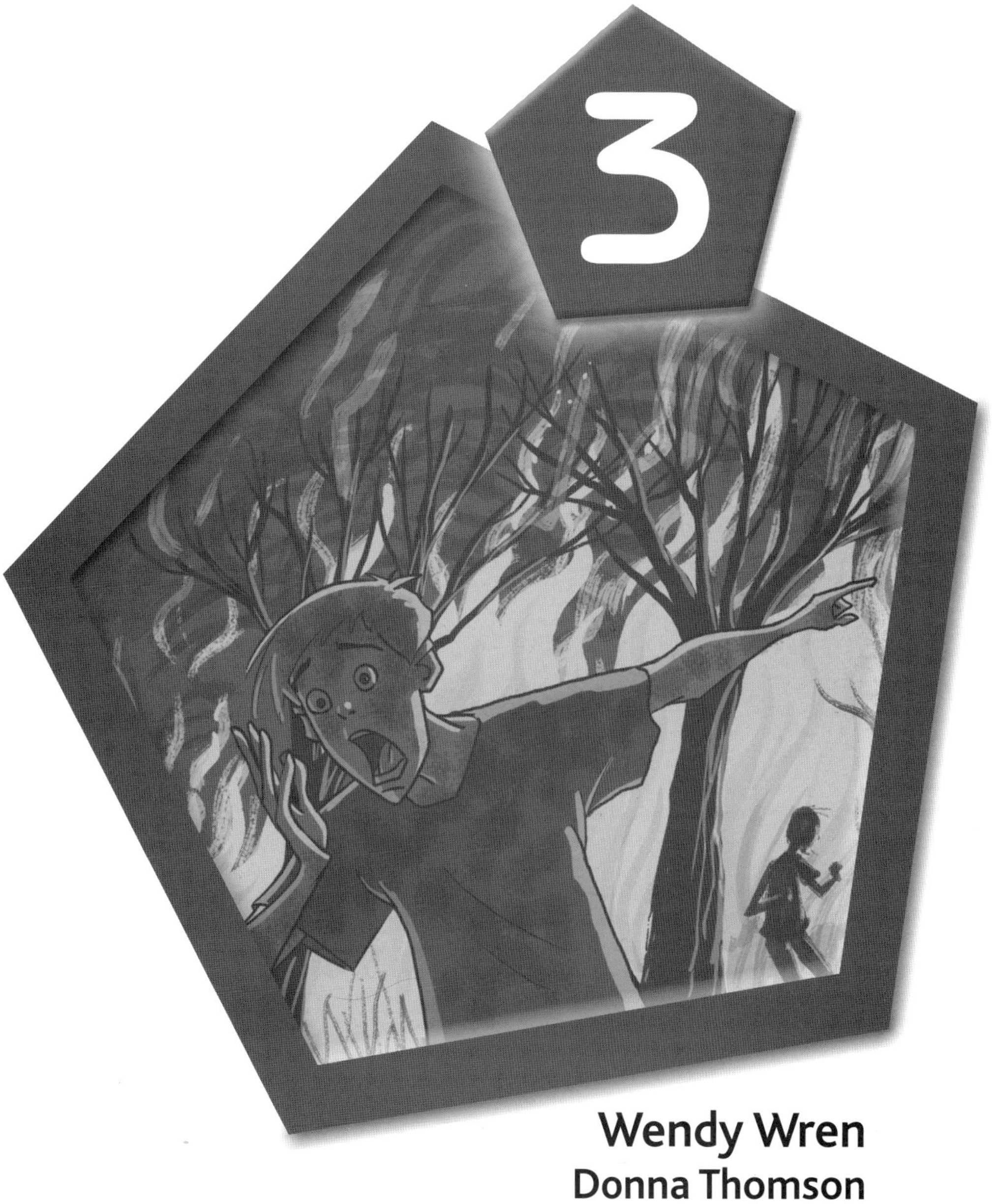

Wendy Wren
Donna Thomson
Doug Dickinson
Series Editor: John Jackman

Nelson Thornes

Published in 2009 by:
Nelson Thornes Ltd
Delta Place
27 Bath Road
CHELTENHAM
GL53 7TH
United Kingdom

09 10 11 12 13 / 10 9 8 7 6 5 4 3 2 1

A catalogue record for this book is available from the British Library

ISBN 978 1 4085 0507 6

Page make-up by Topics – The Creative Partnership, Exeter

Cover illustration by Gustavo Mazali

Printed and bound in Croatia by Zrinski

Pupil Book illustrations by: Gay Galsworthy and Élisabeth Eudes-Pascal at Graham-Cameron Illustration and Robin Edmonds, Gustavo Mazali, Pedro Penizzotto, Norbert Sipos, Studio Pulsar and Roger Wade Walker at Beehive Illustration

Pupil Book photographs courtesy of: Fotolia 24 (all); Getty Images 34, 35, 39, 57; Istock 52 (girl with apple), 53, 56.

Acknowledgements
The author and publisher are grateful to the following for permission to reproduce copyright material:

Cambridge University Press for Eric and Tessa Hadley, 'The Storm' from *Legends of Earth, Air, Fire and Water* by Eric and Tessa Hadley (1985); Express Newspapers for Lucy Johnston and Martyn Halle, 'Outlaw sunbeds plea as cancer cases soar', *Sunday Express*, 16.11.08; A M Heath & Co Ltd on behalf of the Estates of the authors for material from Noel Streatfeild, *The Growing Summer*, Collins (1966). Copyright © Noel Streatfeild 1962; and Joan Aiken, *The Wolves of Willoughby Chase* (1962) pp. 62-3. Copyright © Joan Aiken 1962; Merle Hodge for her story, 'Jeffie Lemmington and Me'; The Orion Publishing Group for material from Lauren St John, *The White Giraffe*, Orion Children's Books (2006) pp. 39-42; Penguin Books Ltd for material from James Vance Marshall, *Walkabout* (first published as *The Children*, Michael Joseph, 1959) pp. 5-6. Copyright © James Vance Marshall 1969; PFD on behalf of the Estate of the author for Hilaire Belloc, 'Jim Who Ran Away From His Nurse' from *Cautionary Verses* by Hilaire Belloc. Copyright © Hilaire Belloc 1907; Martin Reed on behalf of the Estate of the author for Vernon Scannell, 'The Apple Raid'.

Every effort has been made to trace the copyright holders but if any have been inadvertently overlooked the publishers will be pleased to make the necessary arrangements at the first opportunity.

Contents

A Introduction

Reading comprehension has always been a key component in the curriculum of children of all ages, especially children of primary school age. For many years this was seen principally as a means of assessing the extent to which children were truly understanding and interpreting what they had learnt to read. However, more recently, the extent to which developing the skills of reading comprehension can help build all-important thinking skills has become apparent.

While the debate has long been ongoing as to whether spelling is best 'caught or taught', consideration of whether comprehension skills are 'caught or taught' has attracted little or no attention. It seems to have been accepted that if pupils are asked to answer questions on what they have read enough times, they eventually 'get it'. But do they?

Some pupils intuitively understand what they have read on several levels, but the majority of pupils need to be 'taught' these skills in a structured, progressive way. A pupil working individually, reading a passage and answering questions, should be the final, rather than the initial, stage of the process. Helping pupils reach this final stage successfully is the basis for **Nelson Comprehension.**

To read effectively it has been said that pupils should learn to 'read the lines, read between the lines and read beyond the lines'. In other words, they need to acquire a literal understanding of the content, without which they can hardly reach first base. All the class need to be helped and encouraged to achieve this goal. But beyond this, most children should be helped to develop the skills of deduction and inference, whether in understanding a story or in retrieving

information in a non-fiction text, or evaluating or critically analysing what they have read.

We believe that comprehension skills are the essential building blocks of effective learning throughout the curriculum, not just within literacy. They are crucial learning tools in most, if not all, subjects. So, can we risk that children will just 'get it'? We think not!

Nelson Comprehension has therefore been given far more structure and didactic content than previous courses. Each 'unit' in Books 1 to 4 comprises three elements: material devised to support class teaching; followed by group work; and finally offering opportunities for essential individual pupil activity. Unlike other courses, Nelson Comprehension unashamedly teaches comprehension. But, mindful of different requirements within different schools and classes, or even between different children within the same class, the content has been structured to allow flexibility so that, at the extreme, all parts of each unit can be worked through by an individual or small group working together.

To maximise the teaching opportunities, the passages, poems and extracts have been selected to complement requirements of the range of reading required at the relevant stages of the child's development. So, the content is not only appropriate to developing the skills of reading comprehension, but is supportive of other reading and writing requirements.

Nelson Comprehension is also a fully blended series. As well as the exciting and engaging (and fully self-supporting) print resources, the series is complemented with a stunning range of ground-breaking ICT resources in which multimedia (voiceovers, sound effects, film, animations) are used to support comprehension. Not only do these enhance further the teaching and reinforcement of key comprehension skills, they also underline the fact that comprehension skills are as vital as ever in an age of electronic information, such as e-mails, internet, blogs and text messaging.

B How Nelson Comprehension works

Nelson Comprehension works by using a unique three-stage approach to comprehension: starting with teaching key comprehension skills; then moving into pupils' own group discussion and drama activities to reinforce their learning of the key skills; then the final stage where children are presented with a new extract and a set of questions designed to assess what they've learnt.

Planning with Nelson Comprehension

The series covers all six primary year groups (Years 1 to 6, or Scottish P2 to P7) and each year group is split into ten teaching units. These provide coverage of the genres and text types the children are likely to encounter in that particular year: fiction, non-fiction and poetry. Each unit in **Nelson Comprehension** is linked to a specific genre or text type. For example: Year 3 Unit 1 'Familiar places' concerns stories with familiar settings. Within the 'Familiar places' unit, the familiar settings supplied for the extract are home *(The Laughing Snowman)*, the street *(The House of Coloured Windows)* and a new home *(Uninvited Ghosts)*.

Each unit is given a clear main objective, which is identified in the Pupil Book, and full guidance is also given for the *Renewed National Literacy Framework* objectives, *National Curriculum assessment focuses* and the *Scottish Curriculum for Excellence objectives* (see pages 24–27). Further guidance for Wales and Northern Ireland can be found on pages 22–23.

It is not intended that a **Nelson Comprehension** unit forms the basis for a whole framework planning unit which may cover three or four weeks. The work here is very much aimed at the early immersion or analysis phases of a unit of work, in which teaching comprehension skills is of paramount importance, prior to the pupils' planning and composition of their own text in the genre. The extracts are carefully chosen to engage the pupils' interest and maximise teaching and learning opportunities within a class setting. The authors would also recommend the titles from which the extracts are taken for pupils' own reading, or to be used as whole texts for more in-depth study as being excellent examples of the particular genre.

Teach

Each unit is split into three sections: *Teach*, *Talk* and *Write*. All three sections are designed with flexibility in mind, and can be

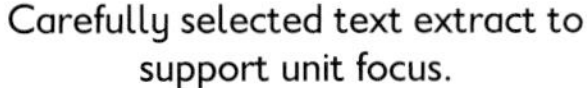
Carefully selected text extract to
support unit focus.

Panel prompts to fully support whole-class and group teaching.

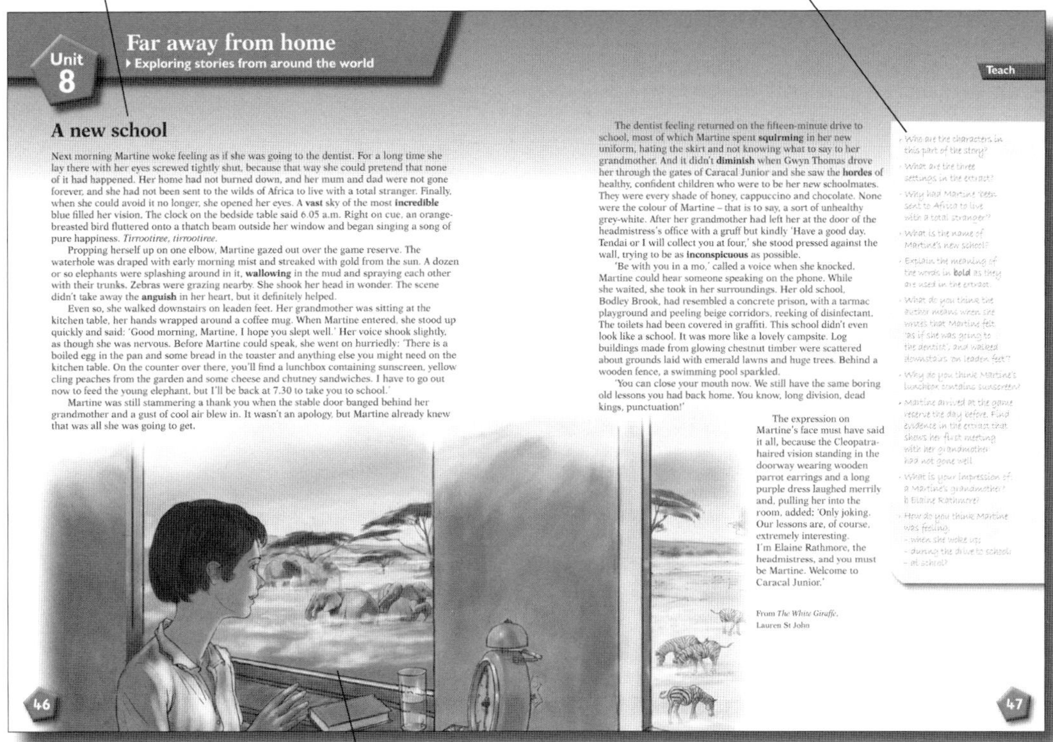

Unit 8

Far away from home

‣ Exploring stories from around the world

Teach

A new school

Next morning Martine woke feeling as if she was going to the dentist. For a long time she lay there with her eyes screwed tightly shut, because that way she could pretend that none of it had happened. Her home had not burned down, and her mum and dad were not gone forever, and she had not been sent to the wilds of Africa to live with a total stranger. Finally, when she could avoid it no longer, she opened her eyes. A **vast** sky of the most **incredible** blue filled her vision. The clock on the bedside table said 6.05 a.m. Right on cue, an orange-breasted bird fluttered onto a thatch beam outside her window and began singing a song of pure happiness. *Tirrootiree, tirrootiree.*

Propping herself up on one elbow, Martine gazed out over the game reserve. The waterhole was draped with early morning mist and streaked with gold from the sun. A dozen or so elephants were splashing around in it, **wallowing** in the mud and spraying each other with their trunks. Zebras were grazing nearby. She shook her head in wonder. The scene didn't take away the **anguish** in her heart, but it definitely helped.

Even so, she walked downstairs on leaden feet. Her grandmother was sitting at the kitchen table, her hands wrapped around a coffee mug. When Martine entered, she stood up quickly and said: 'Good morning, Martine, I hope you slept well.' Her voice shook slightly, as though she was nervous. Before Martine could speak, she went on hurriedly: 'There is a boiled egg in the pan and some bread in the toaster and anything else you might need on the kitchen table. On the counter over there, you'll find a lunchbox containing sunscreen, yellow cling peaches from the garden and some cheese and chutney sandwiches. I have to go out now to feed the young elephant, but I'll be back at 7.30 to take you to school.'

Martine was still stammering a thank you when the stable door banged behind her grandmother and a gust of cool air blew in. It wasn't an apology, but Martine already knew that was all she was going to get.

The dentist feeling returned on the fifteen-minute drive to school, most of which Martine spent **squirming** in her new uniform, hating the skirt and not knowing what to say to her grandmother. And it didn't **diminish** when Gwyn Thomas drove her through the gates of Caracal Junior and she saw the **hordes** of healthy, confident children who were to be her new schoolmates. They were every shade of honey, cappuccino and chocolate. None were the colour of Martine – that is to say, a sort of unhealthy grey-white. After her grandmother had left her at the door of the headmistress's office with a gruff but kindly 'Have a good day. Tendai or I will collect you at four,' she stood pressed against the wall, trying to be as **inconspicuous** as possible.

'Be with you in a mo,' called a voice when she knocked. Martine could hear someone speaking on the phone. While she waited, she took in her surroundings. Her old school, Bodley Brook, had resembled a concrete prison, with a tarmac playground and peeling beige corridors, reeking of disinfectant. The toilets had been covered in graffiti. This school didn't even look like a school. It was more like a lovely campsite. Log buildings made from glowing chestnut timber were scattered about grounds laid with emerald lawns and huge trees. Behind a wooden fence, a swimming pool sparkled.

'You can close your mouth now. We still have the same boring old lessons you had back home. You know, long division, dead kings, punctuation!'

The expression on Martine's face must have said it all, because the Cleopatra-haired vision standing in the doorway wearing wooden parrot earrings and a long purple dress laughed merrily and, pulling her into the room, added: 'Only joking. Our lessons are, of course, extremely interesting. I'm Elaine Rathmore, the headmistress, and you must be Martine. Welcome to Caracal Junior.'

From *The White Giraffe*, Lauren St John

- Who are the characters in this part of the story?
- What are the three settings in the extract?
- Why had Martine been sent to Africa to live with a total stranger?
- What is the name of Martine's new school?
- Explain the meaning of the words in **bold** as they are used in the extract.
- What do you think the author means when she writes that Martine felt 'as if she was going to the dentist', and walked downstairs 'on leaden feet'?
- Why do you think Martine's lunchbox contains sunscreen?
- Martine arrived at the game reserve the day before. Find evidence in the extract that shows her first meeting with her grandmother had not gone well.
- What is your impression of: a Martine's grandmother? b Elaine Rathmore?
- How do you think Martine was feeling:
  - when she woke up;
  - during the drive to school;
  - at school?

46

47

Clear and engaging illustration.

Nelson Comprehension
Pupil Book 3
Unit 8 *Teach*

used in a variety of ways to suit the teachers' needs – whether for use with the whole class, small groups or individually.

The *Teach* section is designed to support whole-class teaching. It provides an illustrated extract and a selection of 'prompt' questions. The teacher and pupils investigate the text using the panel prompts to focus the discussion on the relevant comprehension points/strategies. The teacher then models the strategies required so pupils can understand what is being asked and where and how to answer.

Each *Teach* extract is supplied in the Pupil Book and in this Teacher's Resource Book, where it is fully supported with assessment and answer guidance, and finally as an interactive multi-modal whiteboard version. The whiteboard version of the extract comes complete with questions, set highlights, illustrations, voiceovers, sound effects and, in some cases, animations and video.

The 'questions' in *Teach* are bullet pointed rather than numbered and appear to the right of the text in a 'prompt panel'. The two-page spread has been designed not to look like a typical comprehension exercise but rather as a shared activity where teacher and pupils engage in a class discussion based on the panel prompts.

Carefully selected and illustrated text extract to support group work.

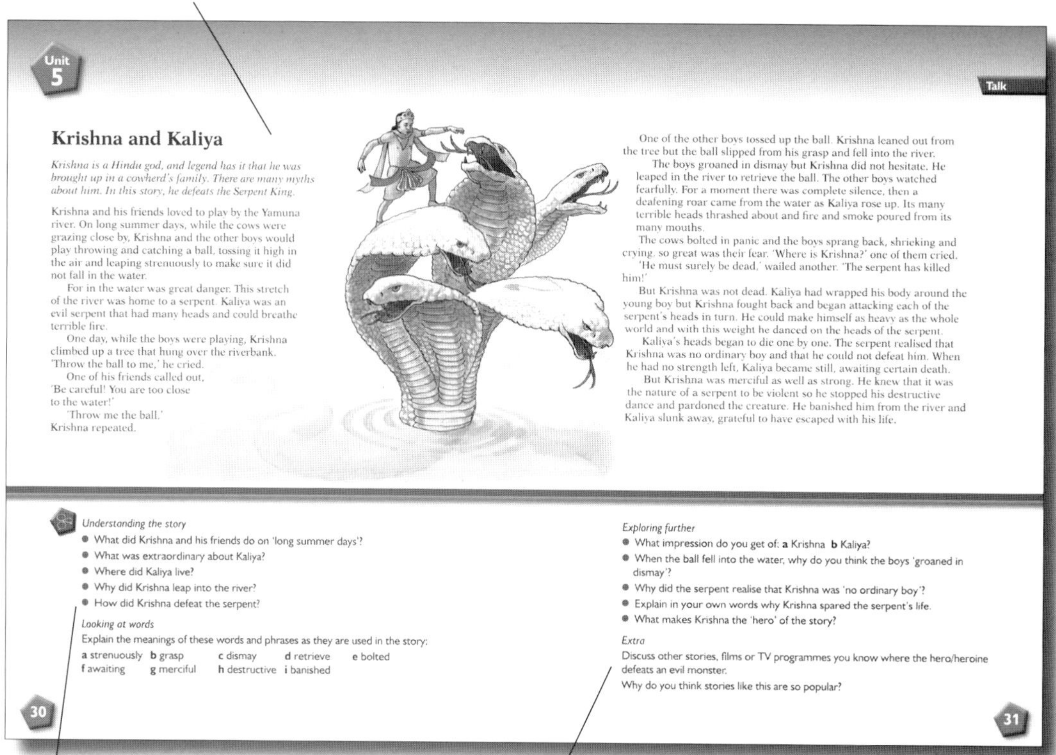

Unit 5

Talk

Krishna and Kaliya

Krishna is a Hindu god, and legend has it that he was brought up in a cowherd's family. There are many myths about him. In this story, he defeats the Serpent King.

Krishna and his friends loved to play by the Yamuna river. On long summer days, while the cows were grazing close by, Krishna and the other boys would play throwing and catching a ball, tossing it high in the air and leaping strenuously to make sure it did not fall in the water.

For in the water was great danger. This stretch of the river was home to a serpent. Kaliya was an evil serpent that had many heads and could breathe terrible fire.

One day, while the boys were playing, Krishna climbed up a tree that hung over the riverbank. 'Throw the ball to me,' he cried.

One of his friends called out, 'Be careful! You are too close to the water!'

'Throw me the ball.' Krishna repeated.

One of the other boys tossed up the ball. Krishna leaned out from the tree but the ball slipped from his grasp and fell into the river.

The boys groaned in dismay but Krishna did not hesitate. He leaped in the river to retrieve the ball. The other boys watched fearfully. For a moment there was complete silence, then a deafening roar came from the water as Kaliya rose up. Its many terrible heads thrashed about and fire and smoke poured from its many mouths.

The cows bolted in panic and the boys sprang back, shrieking and crying, so great was their fear. 'Where is Krishna?' one of them cried.

'He must surely be dead,' wailed another. 'The serpent has killed him!'

But Krishna was not dead. Kaliya had wrapped his body around the young boy but Krishna fought back and began attacking each of the serpent's heads in turn. He could make himself as heavy as the whole world and with this weight he danced on the heads of the serpent.

Kaliya's heads began to die one by one. The serpent realised that Krishna was no ordinary boy and that he could not defeat him. When he had no strength left, Kaliya became still, awaiting certain death.

But Krishna was merciful as well as strong. He knew that it was the nature of a serpent to be violent so he stopped his destructive dance and pardoned the creature. He banished him from the river and Kaliya slunk away, grateful to have escaped with his life.

Understanding the story

- What did Krishna and his friends do on 'long summer days'?
- What was extraordinary about Kaliya?
- Where did Kaliya live?
- Why did Krishna leap into the river?
- How did Krishna defeat the serpent?

Looking at words

Explain the meanings of these words and phrases as they are used in the story:

a strenuously **b** grasp **c** dismay **d** retrieve **e** bolted
f awaiting **g** merciful **h** destructive **i** banished

30

Exploring further

- What impression do you get of: **a** Krishna **b** Kaliya?
- When the ball fell into the water, why do you think the boys 'groaned in dismay'?
- Why did the serpent realise that Krishna was 'no ordinary boy'?
- Explain in your own words why Krishna spared the serpent's life.
- What makes Krishna the 'hero' of the story?

Extra

Discuss other stories, films or TV programmes you know where the hero/heroine defeats an evil monster.

Why do you think stories like this are so popular?

31

Questions arranged according to difficulty in order to support differentiation.

Group presentation activity – usually discussion, drama or composition activity.

Talk

Nelson Comprehension
Pupil Book 3
Unit 5 *Talk*

The *Talk* section is aimed at supporting group work and discussion in order that pupils practise the comprehension strategies taught in *Teach*. A new extract is provided, which the pupils can read in turn, and then a series of questions are given for discussion, starting with literal questions, and then moving on to questions that require more complex comprehension skills, such as inference and evaluation. The final 'Extra' activity is a discussion or drama activity that usually requires the children to work together to produce a performance, or debate a question or issue from the extract, thereby allowing a widening of the scope of the comprehension. This acts as a springboard into personal reflection on what has been read. For example, 'Describe where you live.', 'What do you like about it?', 'What don't you like about it?'

As with *Teach*, each *Talk* extract is supplied in the Pupil Book, Teacher's Resource Book (which supplies full assessment and answer guidance) and for the whiteboard. The whiteboard extract is supported by illustrations and two special 'Talk' activities – interactive activities designed for groups to support the 'Extra' activity.

Questions arranged according to difficulty and colour-coded to support differentiation.

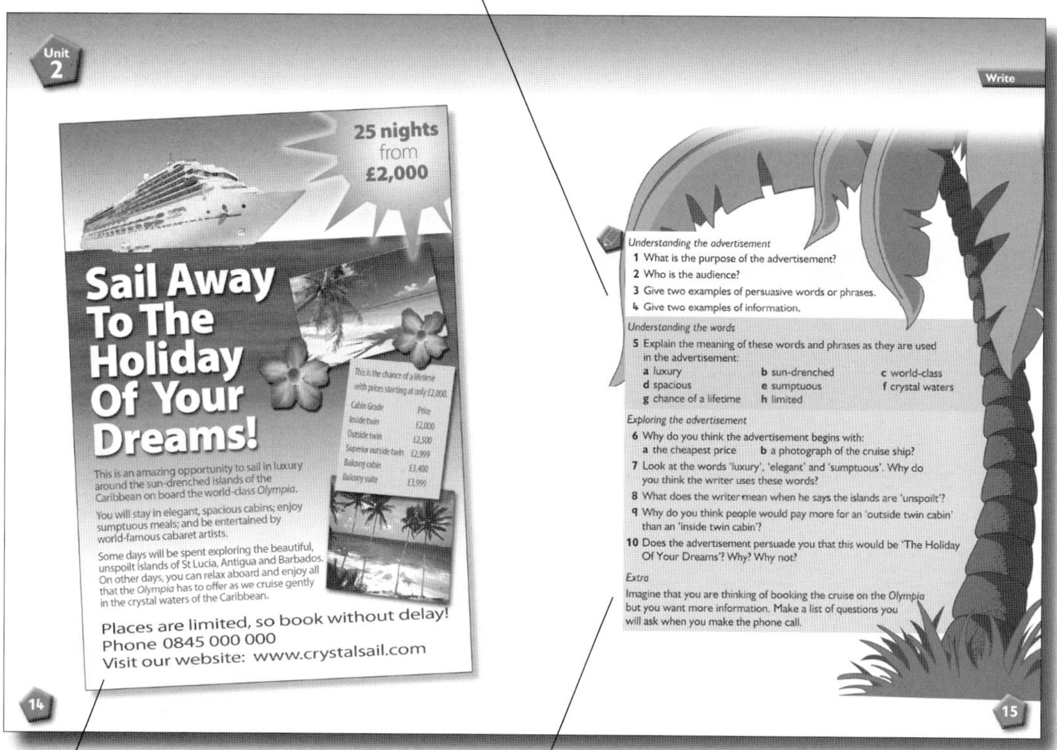

Unit 2

Write

25 nights from £2,000

Sail Away To The Holiday Of Your Dreams!

This is an amazing opportunity to sail in luxury around the sun-drenched islands of the Caribbean on board the world-class *Olympia*.

You will stay in elegant, spacious cabins; enjoy sumptuous meals; and be entertained by world-famous cabaret artists.

Some days will be spent exploring the beautiful, unspoilt islands of St Lucia, Antigua and Barbados. On other days, you can relax aboard and enjoy all that the *Olympia* has to offer as we cruise gently in the crystal waters of the Caribbean.

This is the chance of a lifetime with prices starting at only £2,000.

Cabin Grade	Price
Inside twin	£2,000
Outside twin	£2,500
Superior outside twin	£2,999
Balcony cabin	£3,400
Balcony suite	£3,999

Places are limited, so book without delay!
Phone 0845 000 000
Visit our website: www.crystalsail.com

Understanding the advertisement

1 What is the purpose of the advertisement?
2 Who is the audience?
3 Give two examples of persuasive words or phrases.
4 Give two examples of information.

Understanding the words

5 Explain the meaning of these words and phrases as they are used in the advertisement:
a luxury b sun-drenched c world-class
d spacious e sumptuous f crystal waters
g chance of a lifetime h limited

Exploring the advertisement

6 Why do you think the advertisement begins with:
a the cheapest price b a photograph of the cruise ship?
7 Look at the words 'luxury', 'elegant' and 'sumptuous'. Why do you think the writer uses these words?
8 What does the writer mean when he says the islands are 'unspoilt'?
9 Why do you think people would pay more for an 'outside twin cabin' than an 'inside twin cabin'?
10 Does the advertisement persuade you that this would be 'The Holiday Of Your Dreams'? Why? Why not?

Extra

Imagine that you are thinking of booking the cruise on the *Olympia* but you want more information. Make a list of questions you will ask when you make the phone call.

14 15

New illustrated text extract to support individual oral or written comprehension exercise.

Final extension activity to round off the unit's work.

Write

Nelson Comprehension
Pupil Book 3
Unit 2 *Write*

The *Write* section is aimed at providing individual pupils with the chance to complete a set of comprehension questions so they can be assessed on the strategies they have been taught in *Teach* and *Talk*. While the questions can obviously be used for a full written test, they are also equally ideal for an oral question and answer/discussion activity. The questions are laid out in headed sections with colour banding in order to reflect four different sections (these equate essentially to literal, vocabulary, inference/evaluative and 'Extra') should the teacher wish to set only a part of the whole list of questions, to provide a differentiated task or to fit the time available. Full guidance for assessing the children's responses to the questions is in this Teacher's Resource Book.

An assessment sheet is also provided in this Teacher's Resource Book for each unit's *Write* section, which includes details on the specific question type and National Curriculum assessment focuses used. The assessment sheet (see example overleaf, and pages 88–97) can be used to fully support Assessment for Learning or the Assessing Pupil Progress initiative.

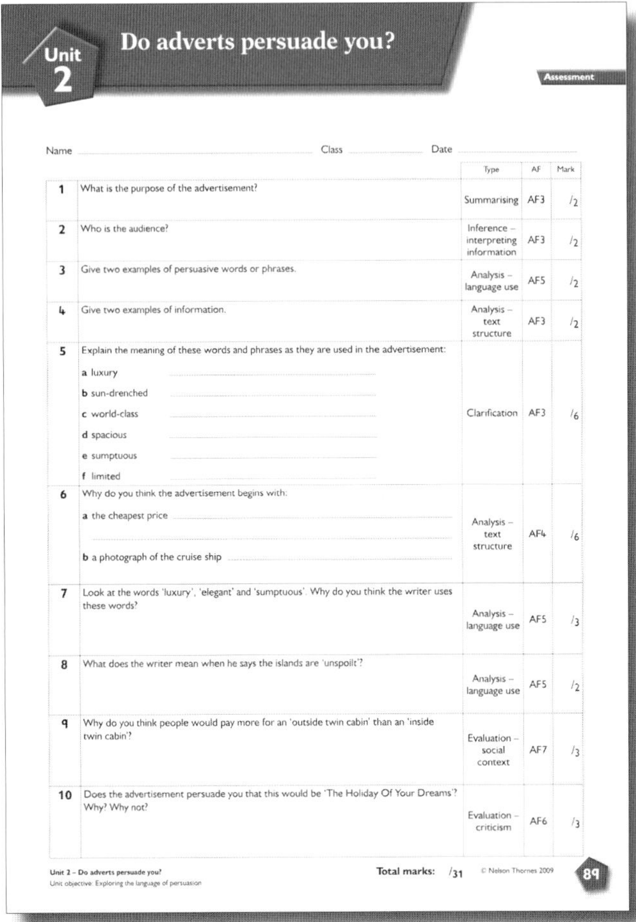

Unit 2

Do adverts persuade you?

Assessment

Name .... Class .... Date ....

		Type	AF	Mark
1	What is the purpose of the advertisement?	Summarising	AF3	/2
2	Who is the audience?	Inference – interpreting information	AF3	/2
3	Give two examples of persuasive words or phrases.	Analysis – language use	AF5	/2
4	Give two examples of information.	Analysis – text structure	AF3	/2
5	Explain the meaning of these words and phrases as they are used in the advertisement: **a** luxury **b** sun-drenched **c** world-class **d** spacious **e** sumptuous **f** limited	Clarification	AF3	/6
6	Why do you think the advertisement begins with: **a** the cheapest price **b** a photograph of the cruise ship	Analysis – text structure	AF4	/6
7	Look at the words 'luxury', 'elegant' and 'sumptuous'. Why do you think the writer uses these words?	Analysis – language use	AF5	/3
8	What does the writer mean when he says the islands are 'unspoilt'?	Analysis – language use	AF5	/2
9	Why do you think people would pay more for an 'outside twin cabin' than an 'inside twin cabin'?	Evaluation – social context	AF7	/3
10	Does the advertisement persuade you that this would be 'The Holiday Of Your Dreams'? Why? Why not?	Evaluation – criticism	AF6	/3

Unit 2 – Do adverts persuade you?
Unit objective: Exploring the language of persuasion

Total marks: /31 © Nelson Thornes 2009 89

Nelson Comprehension
Teacher's Resource Book 3
Unit 2 *Assessment Sheet*

As with *Talk*, an 'Extra' activity is given in *Write*. This is usually a longer written or discussion activity that allows for a widening of the scope of the comprehension, and is a way to reflect and reinforce what has been learnt in the unit. For example:

> Imagine you are Marion or Simon. You are in bed when the ghost comes out of the drawer. Write about:
>
> - what you say
> - what you do
> - how you feel.

Hence, the key pattern for **Nelson Comprehension** is as follows:

- ***Teach:*** Pupils are taught in a whole class situation.
- ***Talk:*** Pupils practise with group support.
- ***Write:*** Pupils do comprehension individually.

Questions and differentiation

The 'prompts' or questions cover lower- and higher-order reading skills. Pupils in all three sections are asked to respond to three basic tiers of questions:

- ***A literal level***, for example, 'What was Mandy going to do if it snowed?'
- ***An inferential level***, for example, 'How do you know that Emma was the only one excited about the snow?'
- ***A personal/evaluative level***, for example, 'How do you feel about snow?'

These three core comprehension skills form the basis of further comprehension skills tested in this series: literal understanding enables information finding and summarising; inference enables interpretation and prediction; evaluation enables criticism, empathy and relating the child's own experience to a particular question or dilemma.

In addition, there is also a vocabulary section to encourage pupils to investigate and clarify the meanings of unknown words in context, using a dictionary if necessary. This strategy unlocks not only the meaning of the word but can have wider implications for the extract as a whole.

The questions in each section are therefore ordered carefully to relate to the ability level of the children, and can be easily broken up into differentiated 'blocks' to fit the needs of a particular ability group.

Introducing and rounding up

The unit notes in the Teacher's Resource Book include suggestions for a 'Before reading' discussion in order to elicit pupils' prior knowledge, thoughts and feelings about an important aspect of the extract or text they are about to read.

Then, after each extract, there is a plenary session (and at the end of each unit, a 'round-up'), which is closely based on class, group or individual work and allows for the reinforcement of comprehension skills and for the unit's key objective.

Picture Snapshot Assessment

A unique further feature of **Nelson Comprehension** is Picture Snapshot Assessment: a ground-breaking method of assessing a pupil's comprehension skills using ICT-based images and animation. This technique is particularly effective with children who are struggling readers, or whose comprehension skills may be masked by problems decoding text. For full details, see pages 98–111).

Glossary of comprehension terms

There are many comprehension terms that relate to the key comprehension strategies. The following are definitions of these terms and are also accompanied by an example of how they might be used as a comprehension question or statement.

Analysis
Identifying and commenting on the organisation, style or features of a text. Understanding the relationship between context, meaning and wording.

The playscript includes a cast list, scene description, character parts and stage directions.

Deduction
Judgement made from inferred clues to form a conclusion.

He realised the show was over when he walked in because he heard applause and saw the actors bowing.

Evaluation – *Personal meaning, empathy, response, opinion*
Looking at 'the bigger picture' – what you think from your own experience that explains the actions, feelings and motives of characters and links to information and mood within a narrative. Expressing and justifying an opinion based on information given.

I think the boy was uneasy about dancing with Emily because he grimaced and stood as far away from her as possible. I say that because the teacher told him to dance with her and Tom didn't like being told what to do. He was also probably embarrassed that the other boys were watching him.

Inference – *Implied and hidden meaning*
Thinking and searching for clues – providing evidence for deductions in answer to questions that ask '*How do you know that*' or '*Why?*' Information that is implied within the text but not given directly, from which connecting evidence is drawn to support deductions.

Q: Can the dragon breathe fire? How do you know?
A: Yes, the dragon can breathe fire because smoke is coming from his nostrils and he has burned the trees next to his lair.

Literal – *Explicit meaning*
Information is obvious and needs no interpretation (Who? What? Where? Right there!). The information is given directly on the page without need for inferring or evaluating to deduce an answer.

Q: What colour is the dragon?
A: The dragon is a bright shade of green.

Clarification – ***Making sense of; making meaning clear***
Defining a word, phrase or concept as it is used in the text. Using appropriate language that accurately and meaningfully describes scenes, events, moods, actions and feelings expressed in a story or non-fiction text when retelling in own words.

Q: 'Use appropriate language that accurately and meaningfully describes scenes and events.' Explain what is meant by 'appropriate language' here.
A: I think 'appropriate language' here means choosing words carefully to convey the same meaning that was used in the text to describe the scenes and events.

Prediction
Anticipating cause and effect from implied, hidden and personal meaning within the text. Giving evidence-based reasons for what you think might have happened before, might be happening now or what might happen next to characters and events in a story.

Q: What will happen next?
A: I think the man walking under the ladder will get covered in paint because the worker above him has just tipped over a tin of paint.

Prior knowledge and experience
Personal history-based understanding, use of what you have already learned or experienced in your own life to predict or explain the meaning of something.

Q: It was a hot spring day on the Cornish coast. Why do you think the boy preferred to stay out of the sea and make sandcastles even though he thought the water looked inviting?
A: I think the boy preferred to stay out of the sea on a hot spring day even though he thought the water looked inviting because he knew that the sea was usually too cold for swimming during springtime in Cornwall.

Summarising / retelling
Gathering, organising and presenting key points of a story or non-fiction information in the correct sequence. Using the basic story structure of beginning, middle and end, a summary or retelling involves a person, action, place, problem and resolution.

The story is about a boy who is playing on a beach in Cornwall on a spring day. He wants to go swimming in the sea but the water is too cold so he makes sandcastles instead.

D Using Nelson Comprehension ICT

Doug Dickinson

Doug Dickinson has worked in primary education for over 40 years, and is currently a lecturer at Leicester University and a primary ICT consultant for a number of primary ICT publishers, having worked for the National Literacy Strategy and Becta.

ICT and comprehension

Since Caxton, ordinary people have been decoding and trying to make sense of the printed word; they have brought their own interpretation to authors' texts and this has led, at times, to some amusing and some disastrous incidents. Today's texts look and feel different; they are not simply composed of words on a page but often come with drawings, photographs and diagrams all interlaced together to form a comprehensive whole.

As we move further into the 21st century, the power of electronic communication in all of our lives becomes more and more evident. Today, many developed texts written to be read for information and for pleasure are multimodal, arriving with the reader in an electronic format that contains all of the printable aspects of the past but also allows for sound, video and animation on pages that can be interrogated, zoomed, hyperlinked. This is a media-rich age, and it is the understanding, the putting into perspective and the dealing with the inferences of the texts presented that is the current life skill of comprehension.

It is the comprehension (the understanding) of all of these types of text that is the function of this exciting software package, which comes complete with age-grouped examples to help readers get the best out of the fiction and non-fiction that influences and excites their learning and recreation.

Teach

The aim of the *Teach* section is to provide a teacher with fully interactive whiteboard support for the teaching of key comprehension skills.

Each *Teach* section contains an illustrated extract, which comes with click-on highlights and question boxes. Each highlight either specifically answers the particular question or, in the case of an inference question, provides clues before offering possible answers/free type for the teacher (thereby offering a three-stage process: question – clues – possible answers; this is vital for teaching children inference, deduction and 'reading between the lines').

Teachers can also make their own annotations on the extract by using their own interactive whiteboard tools or the tools provided.

The readers engage with the quality text, perhaps in a whole class or group setting, or as a guided read displayed on an interactive whiteboard. Using the annotation tools (which dock to the left of the text, but which can also be moved to any position on the screen), the text can be explained and key points emphasised.

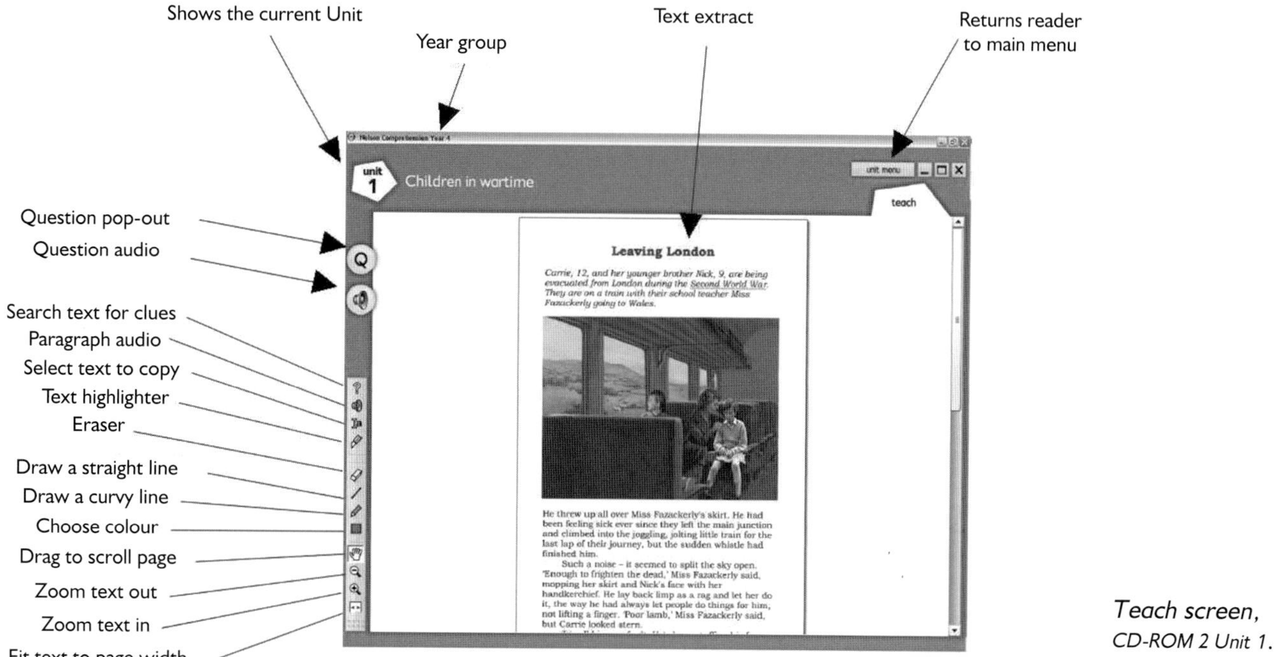

Teach screen,
CD-ROM 2 Unit 1.

The questions for comprehension are accessed by clicking the 'Question pop-out'. Each question is intended to guide a reader towards understanding of the text by requiring one of a range of comprehension skills, such as literal understanding, inference, deduction or evaluation. Clues within the text can be accessed (and become highlighted in the text) by clicking on the 'Show clue' button.

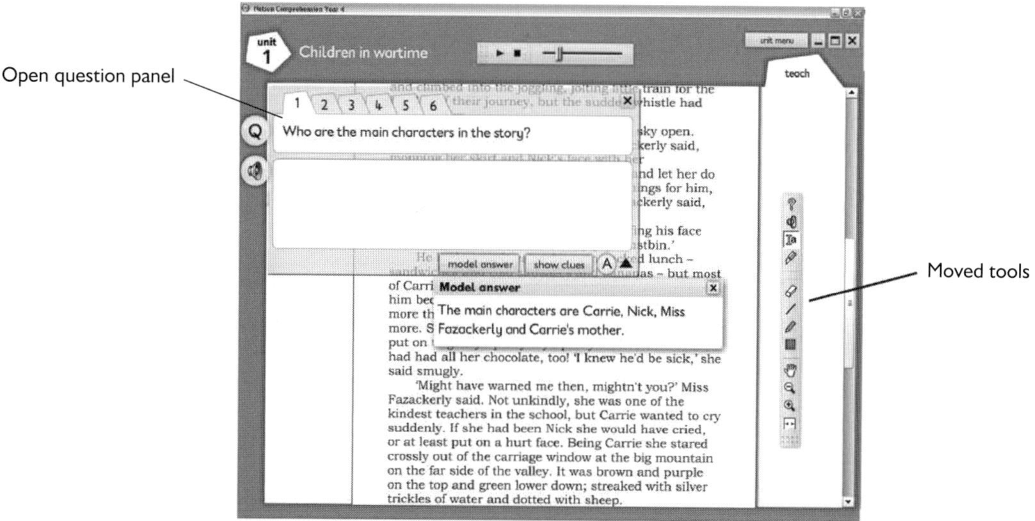

Answers to the questions can be inputted into the answer panel by clicking on the 'A' button. This opens a free writing panel. It is possible to copy and paste from the text into this panel if this is appropriate. A model answer is available for each question by clicking on the 'Model answer' button. This is intended as a guide and isn't necessarily the only answer – certainly, evaluation questions may well induce very different but equally plausible answers.

This *Teach* page has the capacity to utilise many multimedia functions to further learning and enrich comprehension (or to provide visual and audio to support a struggling reader). For example, the picture or the words can be toggled on or off (using the button in the bottom right of the picture or in the top left for the words), the sound can be switched on or off, and various other electronic supports, by way of video and animation, can all assist in the comprehension of the whole text. This multimedia provision facilitates different 'layers' of meaning – so, by adding or taking away images, voiceover or sound effects, a passage can be made easier, more difficult, or more accessible to children with different learning styles or to struggling readers with strong thinking skills.

Talk

The aim of the Talk section is to provide activities for children to work on in small groups – providing a stimulus for speaking and listening, drama and discussion – in order to reinforce important comprehension skills.

This section offers a new illustrated text extract and breakout activities for pairs and small groups of children to engage in supported and motivating discussion/ role play/drama scenarios, based on a static extract screen (which may have illustrations). This is clearly a 'speaking and listening' activity.

The different activities can be amended (with imported assets or typed over script) in order to make work more or less challenging, or perhaps to fit a different piece of text.

Character / object grid (including thesaurus)

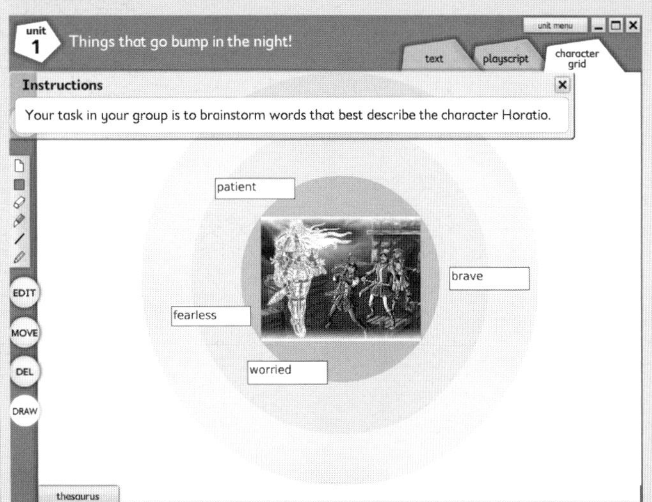

The 'Character grid' gives an opportunity for a group or class to develop vocabulary to describe characters in the text and place them within zones of relevance. By doing so, it stimulates the children to explore key characters, to empathise with their situation, to evaluate their character within the story, as well as to extend their descriptive vocabulary. The grid is also used with story settings and objects of inherent importance to the texts.

The top four buttons on the default toolbar allow users to move between edit, move and interact, delete, and draw and annotate functions. Each function has its separate set of extra tools to add exciting, personalised dimensions to the activity.

The excellent 'Media bank' is accessed from the 'edit' toolbar.

Another feature available from the 'Media bank' which allows for creativity in this section is the 'avatar maker'. Accessing this allows users to create and mould their own characters to be represented in the 'Character grid'.

The 'Character grid' also has a 'thesaurus' tool, which supports users in selecting appropriate words for the zones. Words from the thesaurus can be copied and pasted into a zone or it can be searched for suitable synonyms, thus extending user vocabulary.

The main text for the activity can always be accessed for reference by clicking on the text tab.

Story map

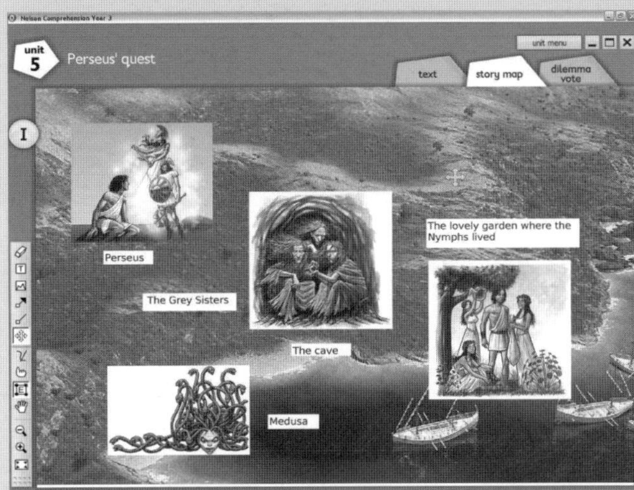

The 'Story map' uses similar functionality to the 'Character grid'. It allows users to review the text, identifying key events in sequence, and confirm their understanding by annotating the adjustable text blocks. It can also be used like a diagram with label and caption boxes.

Question maker

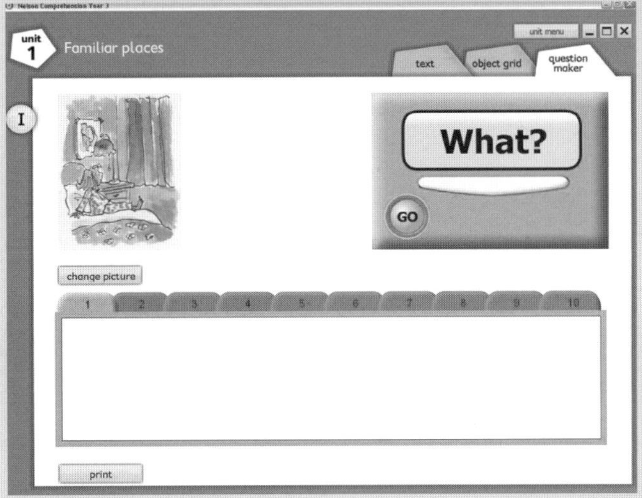

The 'Question maker' allows users to generate questions about characters and situations. The 'questioners' use the 'I' button on the screen to get instructions about the activity, together with the 'question generator' (which provides the 'Who?', 'What?', 'How?', 'Why?', 'When?' and 'Where?' question starters). They type their questions into the answer boxes (clicking on the tabs in turn) and then the character, in role, provides the answers. The skill of creating the right questions to find the information or answers they wish to know is of immense importance in developing key comprehension skills.

Each unit that utilises the 'Question maker' has its own set of instructions providing range and depth of activity.

Dilemma vote

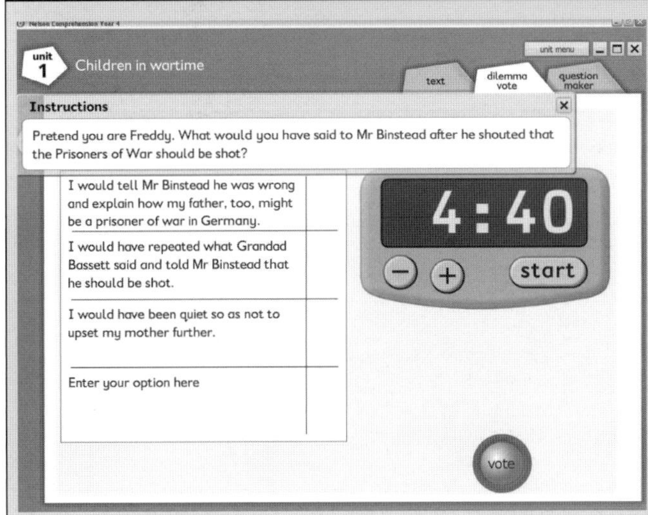

The readers are presented with a dilemma from a new text which they discuss and then vote on several options. There is a 'free type' option to give the group the opportunity to develop their own ideas. The dilemma could involve prediction, or evaluating and giving an opinion, or using inference to deduce an answer.

The default time for discussion is set to five minutes but this can be altered to suit the local situation.

In a class situation, the groups decide if they want to add another option and, once this has been agreed, start the timer and discuss the dilemma. Ideally, some of these discussions could be digitally recorded so that the quality of the discussion could be reviewed and each person's part in it evaluated. This would also support the collection of evidence of speaking and listening for APP (Assessing Pupil Progress).

When the discussion time is ended the individuals in the group then vote on their personal choice of solution to the dilemma. The idea is that they vote based on the arguments they have heard in the discussion time. To vote they simply click on the 'vote' button and the 'ballot box' will appear. They then place their 'X' next to their choice of solution and click the 'ballot box' again. An animation will show that their vote has been cast! To see how the votes add up simply click on the 'chart' button.

Info categoriser / Sequencer

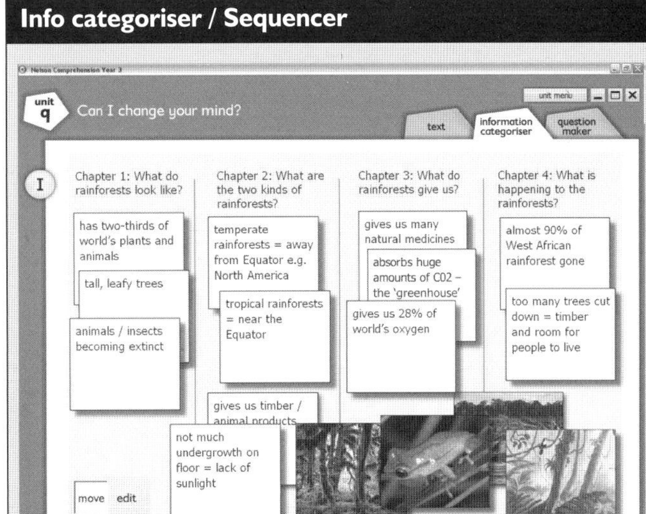

Info categoriser

This amazingly powerful application allows users to organise their knowledge gained from their understanding of the text. Each of the prepared facts or images can be edited and placed into the frameworks provided. The boxes can be edited, so the 'Info categoriser' can actually be used as a planning or research tool for further written work. As a tool it is ideal as a means to test a pupil's ability to analyse and organise information.

Clicking on the 'I' button gives instructions for the activity.

Sequencer

The 'Sequencer' allows users to do exactly what it says – sequence events or ideas in words or pictures. It can be effectively used as a full-scale writing planner. Each of the items already added to the sequence can be edited and moved by accessing the buttons on the bottom right of the screen and extra items can be added into the blanks provided. Like the 'Info categoriser', the edit feature takes the activity beyond sequencing, allowing its use as a text planning tool, or as a way to retell or summarise a text extract. Clicking on the 'I' button gives instructions for each unit activity.

Media bank

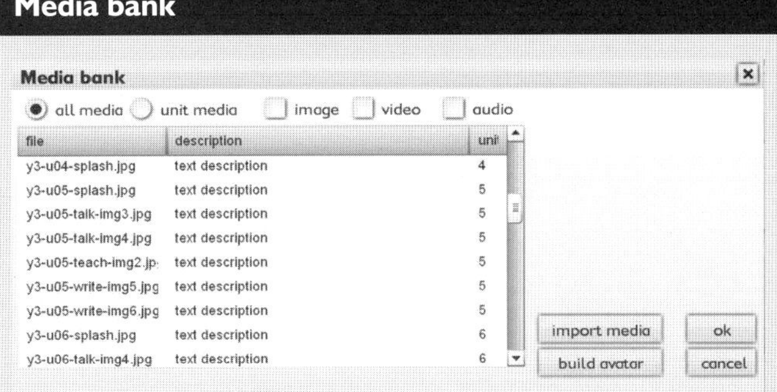

By clicking on the 'change picture' button (in the 'Question maker') or on the 'Media bank' icon (on the 'Character grid') a media bank is accessed, which allows for a variety of media types to be displayed in the 'Question maker' window. It is possible here to access all media from all installed units, or just the media for the displayed unit. Buttons on the bottom right of the 'Media bank' allow for personal media to be imported, such as an image or a film.

Text formatter

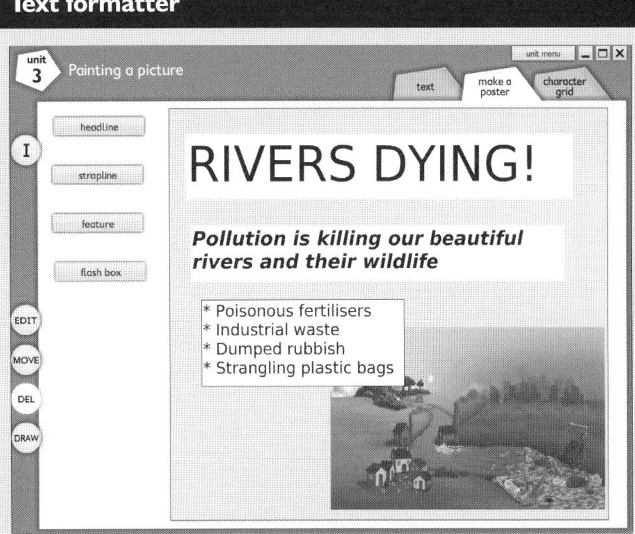

Make a playscript, Write a letter, Write insructions, Make an advert, Make an explanation, Make a poster

The 'Text formatter' allows users to create text-based contexts where the focus is on the quality of the literacy expressed through an understanding of the genre and the context of the unit. In the case of 'Make a playscript' the options allow a child to do just that, by providing playscript blocks on demand (for example, cast lists, scene descriptions and dialogue) so the child can focus on creating the content – whether it's transforming a prose passage into a playscript or creating another scene of the playscript.

The other text formatters work in a similar way and also allow the importation, through the 'Media bank', of images for illustration, which are particularly important in the case of 'Make an advert' or 'Make a poster'. The 'Text formatter' is ideal to support a child in understanding and analysing the organisation and structure of different text types.

Supporting assessment with Talk *activities*

Talk activity	Comprehension skills	Related AFs
Dilemma vote	prediction; inference; evaluation – opinion, empathy; historical/cultural context	AF2, AF3, AF6, AF7
Character/object grid	analysis – language use; evaluation – opinion, empathy; historical/ cultural context	AF5, AF7
Question maker	literal; inference; evaluation	AF2, AF3, AF6
Info categoriser	inference; analysis – text structure	AF3, AF4
Sequencer	summarising; analysis – text structure	AF2, AF4
Story	map visualisation; summarising; analysis – text structure	AF2, AF4
Text formatter	analysis – text structure/language use; inference; prediction; evaluation	AF3, AF4, AF5, AF6

Write

The aim of this section is to provide a means of reviewing the Pupil Book Write activities as a class/group in order to reinforce and build on the skills taught and learnt in the unit as a whole. This section is provided with a separate, but complementary, illustrated text (which can also be used as a teaching tool if teachers prefer) with around 10 questions of different types. The focus here, as in Teach, is on the use of the extract–questions–clues–blank–model answer sequence as a way of reviewing the children's written or even oral answers.

The tools available are complementary to those available in the Teach section of each unit, so as well as the 10 set questions (with highlights and clues) there is the option for the teacher or a pupil to make their own annotations and highlights on the text extract.

Picture Snapshot Assessment

The 'Picture Snapshot Assessment' is an exclusively electronic means of assessing a struggling reader's comprehension and thinking skills using visual images or animations (often accompanied by audio effects) as a basis for questions. This section is also supplied with an assessment tool that can be used as a basis for future planning for an individual pupil's needs.

The assessments here are based on users showing their ability to comprehend and answer questions that demonstrate literal, evaluation, inference, prediction and classification understanding. A simple summary is available of the results to sit alongside the evidence gathered for APP. For full details of the 'Picture Snapshot Assessment', see pages 98–111 of this book.

E Nelson Comprehension and Assessment for Learning

Donna Thomson

Comprehension is a fundamental component of reading. Children need to understand that alongside 'accurate decoding of text', 'reading involves making meaning from content, structure and language' (QCA, 2006). However, children do not learn these skills without instruction. To become fluent readers they must not only be taught how to decode words accurately but also learn how to understand and interpret the author's meaning.

Assessing Pupil Progress

Comprehension assessment provides teachers with a wealth of information and is central to effective teaching and learning. The primary purpose for asking readers a range of comprehension questions is to find out what they need to be taught to support their understanding of text. Comprehension assessment offers teachers an insight into a reader's depth of thinking during and after reading. It tells them whether they are making sense of incoming information; whether they are able to infer, evaluate and justify responses to questions about the text; and how much they understand and are able to personally relate to the author's meaning.

The assessment focus (AF) criteria used to help teachers to assess pupil's reading progress clearly reflect the importance of comprehension in the development of good reading skills. Six out of the seven National Strategy assessment focuses refer to comprehension competencies and are directly linked to the criterion of National Curriculum levels (see the National Strategy grid).

Assessing Pupil Progress (APP) provides teachers with an effective structure for tracking children's learning and helps them to tailor their teaching to meet the needs of developing readers. It helps teachers to identify weaknesses and strengths through day-to-day and periodic assessment in relation to specific assessment focuses, and enables them to monitor the impact teaching and planning from AF evidence has on other areas of the pupils' learning. Intervention using these indicators raises standards of attainment in reading and across the curriculum, which in turn improves SATs results and ensures that children experience a smoother transition to secondary education.

Gathering assessment focus evidence for APP

Children's written responses to comprehension provide easy access to AF evidence. The Nelson Comprehension series provides a focus for this evidence using a range of quality extracts and carefully thought-out questions that support the teaching of the comprehension strategies.

However, in practice much of the evidence that is gathered in order to check a child's reading level and progression occurs in passing, through discussion and questioning about texts – particularly in Key Stage 1.

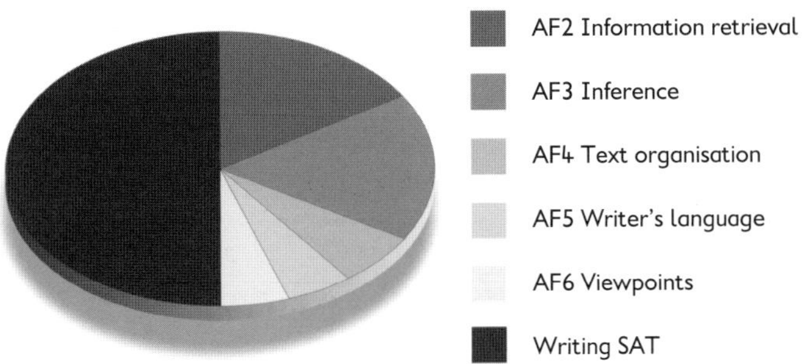

2008 SATs
Marks break-down

The range of extracts and activities within the Nelson Comprehension series offer an excellent opportunity for discussion and oral responses to questions, particularly the *Teach* and *Talk* sections. Guided and shared reading offer valuable opportunities for teachers to explore a range of fiction and non-fiction through discussion and questions that help to develop and monitor children's understanding of text. Another activity that guides and develops comprehension is Reciprocal Reading (Palicsar and Brown, 1986), recommended by the Revised National Strategy, 2006. The 'Picture Snapshot Assessment' (see the CD-ROMs and pages 98–111 of this book) offers a means of building these skills.

Other speaking and listening activities that enable teachers to assess children's comprehension on a day-to-day basis are as follows:

- retelling from stories, a newspaper report or instructions, etc., where children are required to select the main ideas, sequence them correctly and say them coherently in their own words (AFs 2, 3, 4)
- drama, where children re-enact something they have read that relies on gathering and organising key information, interpretation and sequencing skills (AFs 2, 3, 4)
- 'hot-seating', where children act out characters from a story and others ask them questions that they need to answer in character role – in as much detail as possible – which draws on main and inferred ideas from story, interpretation of character and ideas, deduction and reference to text (AFs 2, 3, 4, 6).

There are examples of all these types of activity within the Nelson Comprehension series, and these are supported by the ICT Talk activities on the CD-ROM – such as the sequencer, the info categoriser, the dilemma vote and the question maker (for more details see 'Using Nelson Comprehension ICT' on pages 14–19).

Assessment focuses are also linked to different types of comprehension question and answer. For example, literal questions ask the children to locate the main 'who?', 'what?', 'where?' information from text to answer questions (AF2). Inference questions ask children to infer, deduce and provide evidence for their answers from text (AF3). Evaluation questions ask the children to empathise with characters using their own life experience and knowledge to explain the characters' behaviour or possible motives (AF6), and clarification questions ask about vocabulary and the author's use of language (AF3 and AF5).

Each unit comes with its own assessment grid, providing the 'Write' questions and activities along with guidance on question type, relevant assessment focus and a helpful marking system that can help inform your judgement on how well a child is using his/her comprehension skills. These can be found on pages 88–97 of this Teacher's Resource Book.

AF	AF description	Skills covered
AF2	Understand, describe, select or retrieve information, events or ideas from texts and use quotation and reference to text	literal, information finding, summarising
AF3	Deduce, infer or interpret information, events or ideas from texts	visualisation, inference, deducing information, prediction, clarification, drawing on prior knowledge
AF4	Identify and comment on the structure and organisation of texts, including grammatical and presentational features at text level	analysis of text structure
AF5	Explain and comment on writers' uses of language, including grammatical and literary features at word and sentence level	analysis of language use
AF6	Identify and comment on writers' purposes and viewpoints, and the overall effect of the text on the reader	evaluation – empathy, author viewpoint, opinion, criticism, previous experience
AF7	Relate texts to their social, cultural and historical contexts and literary traditions	evaluation – social, cultural, geographical and historical contexts

Full reading assessment guidelines are supplied on the DCSF Standards site.

Although reading and written comprehension is key to assessing children's depth of thinking, range of vocabulary and understanding of text, there are a number of children this does not suit because they struggle when decoding words on the page. They may have good inference skills, a rich verbal vocabulary and impressive understanding of the author's intention in discussion about text that has been read to them. However, these high-level skills are unlikely to be reflected in their responses to questions when they have had to read the text by themselves. As a result, they are likely to be assessed as 'poor' readers when it is actually their decoding that has failed at this level, rather than their 'whole' reading ability. It is important, therefore, that pupils can be assessed as much for their ability to infer, evaluate and comprehend the author's meaning, as they are for their decoding ability.

Nelson Comprehension's 'Snapshot Assessment' (see pages 98–111) offers an innovative solution to the problem of assessing the comprehension skills of struggling decoders. It also provides an effective comprehension measure for more able decoders who may already be assumed to be 'good readers' simply on the basis that they have fluent word recognition.

Using Nelson Comprehension with other curricula

Assessment for Learning and reading comprehension are at the heart of all the primary national curricula. As well as the English Primary National Literacy Strategy and Assessing Pupil Progress, the Scottish Curriculum for Excellence, the revised Northern Irish Curriculum for Key Stages 1 and 2, and the new

Welsh Key Stage 1 and 2 Curriculum all emphasise the need for the following key elements of assessment for learning:

- Sharing learning intentions with the children.
- Using day-to-day observation, along with discussion, oral activities and written activities, when assessing a child's comprehension skills.
- Adjusting teaching according to each child's assessment needs arising from these formative assessments.

Northern Ireland Key Stage 2 objectives	English Guidance for Key Stage 2 (Wales)
Talking and Listening Nelson Comprehension offers opportunities to engage with the following objectives: • Listening and responding to a range of fiction, poetry, drama and media texts. • Group and class discussions for a variety of purposes – responding to and evaluating ideas, arguments and points of view. • Telling, retelling and interpreting stories based on personal experiences and literature.	Nelson Comprehension supports the following lines of progression for: ***Oracy*** *Listening with understanding* (levels 1 to 5) – from paying attention to what is said to responding with questions and comments and more perceptive contributions. *Participation in discussion* (levels 1 to 6) – from taking part in a conversation to managing turn-taking and intervening, listening to others and taking account of discussion. *Expressing opinion* (levels 3 to 6) – from expressing opinion simply, developing response and justifying opinion offering evidence and with sensitivity to others.
Reading Nelson Comprehension offers opportunities to engage with the following objectives: • Reading and exploring a range of traditional and electronic texts, using drama, art and discussion to focus on distinctive features. • Representing stories and information texts in a range of visual forms and diagrams. • Justifying responses logically, by inference, deduction or reference to evidence within the text. • Discussing and considering aspects of stories, for example themes, characters, plots, places, objects and events. • Begin to be aware of how different media present information, ideas and events in different ways.	***Reading*** *Reading increasingly demanding texts* (levels 1 to 5) – developing independent reading, using appropriate reading strategies and understanding texts of increasing length, complexity and sophistication. *Response to texts, including analysing and evaluating* (levels 1 to 6) – from simple likes and dislikes, to supporting preferences with reference to texts; identifying and responding to key features of texts, and critically appreciate texts. *Reading for information* (levels 1 to 6) – from locating information for a specific purpose, to collecting and synthesising for different purposes; developing appropriate reading strategies (skimming and scanning).
Writing Nelson Comprehension offers opportunities to engage with the following objectives: • Discuss various features of layout in texts which they are reading, so they can use them in their own writing.	

For links to the Renewed Primary Literacy Framework and the Scottish Curriculum for Excellence, please see individual unit descriptions.

F Nelson Comprehension unit by unit

Unit	Unit name	Skills	Genre/text type	Extracts	Renewed framework objectives
1	Trouble for Oliver!	Understanding the layout and conventions of playscripts	Playscripts	*Oliver asks for more* *Oliver and the undertaker* *Oliver meets the Artful Dodger* (All based on *Oliver Twist* by Charles Dickens)	**3** *Group discussion and interaction* • Understand different ways to take the lead and support others in groups. **4** *Drama* • Perform a scripted scene making use of dramatic conventions. • Use and recognise the impact of theatrical effects in drama. **5** *Engaging with and responding to texts* • Explore how writers use language for comic and dramatic effects.
2	Do adverts persuade you?	Exploring the language of persuasion	Adverts	*The power of advertising* *The copywriter's job* *Sail Away To The Holiday Of Your Dreams!*	**1** *Speaking* • Present a spoken argument, sequencing points logically, defending views with evidence, and making use of persuasive language. **2** *Listening and responding* • Analyse the use of persuasive language. **3** *Group discussion and interaction* • Plan and manage a group task over time using different levels of planning. • Understand different ways to take the lead and support others in groups. **7** *Understanding and interpreting texts* • Use evidence from across a text to explain events or ideas. • Infer writers' perspectives from what is written and what is implied. • Explore how writers use language for dramatic effects.
3	Understanding character	Exploring characters' points of view and feelings	Novels focusing on character	*The Growing Summer* Noel Streatfeild *The Wolves of Willoughby Chase* Joan Aiken *Ash Road* Ivan Southall	**7** *Understanding and interpreting texts* • Infer writer's perspectives from what is written and what is implied. • Explore how writers use language for comic and dramatic effects.
4	Technology know-how	Understanding the features of instructions	Instructions	*How to use Booksbooks – your online bookshop* *How to download photographs to your desktop* *Alarm clock*	**7** *Understanding and interpreting texts* • Compare different types of information texts and identify how they are structured. **8** *Engaging with and responding to texts* • Compare the usefulness of techniques such as visualisation. **9** *Creating and shaping texts* • Create multi-layered texts, including use of hyperlinks, linked with web pages. **11** *Sentence structure and punctuation* • Adapt sentence construction to different text types, purposes and readers.
5	Heroes and villains	Understanding the roles of heroes and heroines	Traditional stories, fables, myths and legends	*King Arthur and His Knights* Anonymous *Krishna and Kaliya* *'The Storm'* from *Legends of Earth, Air, Fire and Water* Eric and Tessa Hadley	**3** *Group discussion and interaction* • Plan and manage a group task over time using different levels of planning. **4** *Drama* • Reflect on how working in role helps to explore complex issues. **7** *Understanding and interpreting texts* • Use evidence from across a text to explain events or ideas. **8** *Engaging with and responding to texts* • Use techniques such as visualisation, prediction and empathy in exploring the meaning of texts.

Scottish C for E objectives	NC assessment focuses	Comprehension skills	ICT Talk activities
Listening and Talking *Understanding, analysing and evaluating (third level)* Show understanding of what is listened to or watched by commenting, with evidence, on the content and form of short and extended texts. **Reading** *Finding and using information (third and fourth levels)* Able to make notes and organise them to develop thinking, help retain and recall information, explore issues, and create new texts (using own words as appropriate).	AF2, AF4	***Literal*** – finding information ***Inference*** – interpreting information ***Clarification*** ***Evaluation*** – empathy, personal experience, historical context	Character grid Text formatter (playscript)
Listening and Talking *Understanding, analysing and evaluating (third level)* Develop an informed view through learning about the techniques used to influence opinion; learn how to assess the value of different sources, and recognise persuasion. **Reading** *Understanding, analysing and evaluating (third level)* Develop an informed view through learning about techniques used to influence opinion; learn to recognise persuasion, and assess the reliability of information from different sources.	AF5, AF6	***Inference*** – interpreting information ***Analysis*** – language use, text structure ***Clarification*** ***Evaluation*** – social context, criticism	Information categoriser Text formatter (advert)
Listening and Talking *Tools for listening and talking (third level)* Make relevant contributions when engaging with others, encourage others to contribute and acknowledge that they have the right to hold a different opinion. **Reading** *Enjoyment and choice (third and fourth levels)* Give reasons, with evidence, for their personal responses.	AF3, AF6	***Literal*** – finding information ***Clarification*** ***Inference*** – interpreting information ***Evaluation*** – empathy	Character grid Dilemma vote
Listening and Talking *Finding and using information (third level)* Can identify and give an accurate account of the purpose of the text; identify and discuss similarities between different types of text and use this information for different purposes. **Reading** *Finding and using information (third and fourth levels)* Can use knowledge of features of different types of text to find, select, sort, summarise, link and use information from different sources.	AF4, AF5	***Literal*** – finding information ***Analysis*** – text structure ***Evaluation*** – personal experience, criticism	Question maker Information categoriser
Listening and Talking *Creating texts (third level)* Develop confidence when engaging with others, and communicate in a clear and expressive way. **Reading** *Understanding, analysing and evaluating (third and fourth levels)* Identify and discuss similarities and differences between texts, and compare and contrast different texts.	AF3, AF7	***Literal*** – finding information ***Clarification*** ***Evaluation*** – empathy, social context ***Analysis*** – language use ***Evaluation*** – empathy	Dilemma vote Text formatter (playscript)

Unit	Unit name	Skills	Genre/text type	Extracts	Renewed framework objectives
6	Digging for the past	Exploring the use of recount in the media	Recount	*An Egyptian Treasure* *Treasures of the past* *The Valley of the Kings*	**3** *Group discussion and interaction* • Plan and manage a group task over time using different levels of planning. • Understand different ways to take the lead and support others in groups. • Understand the process of decision making. **7** *Understanding and interpreting texts* • Use evidence from across a text to explain events or ideas.
7	Let me tell you a story	Telling stories through poetry	Narrative poetry	*Jim – Who Ran Away From His Nurse, And Was Eaten By A Lion* Hilaire Belloc, from *Cautionary Tales for Children* *The Apple-Raid* Vernon Scannell *Early Last Sunday Morning* Ian Souter	**3** *Group discussion and interaction* • Plan and manage a group task over time using different levels of planning. • Understand different ways to take the lead and support others in groups. • Understand the process of decision making. **4** *Drama* • Reflect on how working in role helps to explore complex issues. **7** *Understanding and interpreting texts* • Use evidence from across a text to explain events or ideas. • Explore how writers use language for comic and dramatic effect. **8** *Engaging with and responding to texts* • Compare how a common theme is presented in poetry.
8	Far away from home	Exploring stories from around the world	Novels about other cultures	*The White Giraffe* Lauren St John *Jeffie Lemmington and Me* Merle Hodge *Walkabout* James Vance Marshall	**3** *Group discussion and interaction* • Understand different ways to take the lead and support others in groups. **4** *Drama* • Reflect on how working in role helps to explore complex issues. **7** *Understanding and interpreting texts* • Use evidence from across a text to explain events or ideas. • Infer writer's (character's) perspective from what is written and what is implied.
9	Fantasy landscapes	Exploring persuasive language	Persuasive texts – letters and articles	*You Are What You Eat* *Letter commenting on 'You Are What You Eat'* *Outlaw sunbeds plea as cases of skin cancer soar* Sunday Express	**1** *Speaking* • Present a spoken argument, sequencing points logically, defending views with evidence, and making use of persuasive language. **2** *Listening and responding* • Analyse the use of persuasive language. **3** *Group discussion and interaction* • Plan and manage a group task over time using different levels of planning. • Understand different ways to take the lead and support others in groups. **7** *Understanding and interpreting texts* • Use evidence from across the text to explain events or ideas. • Infer writers' perspectives from what is written and what is implied. • Explore how writers use language for dramatic effects.
10	Long, long ago	Exploring older novels	Stories written in the early 20th century and before	*The Railway Children* E. Nesbit *Little Women* Louisa May Alcott *The Secret Garden* Frances Hodgson Burnett	**3** *Group discussion and interaction* • Plan and manage a group task over time using different levels of planning. **4** *Drama* • Reflect on how working in role helps to explore complex issues. **7** *Understanding and interpreting texts* • Use evidence from the across a text to explain events or ideas. **8** *Engaging with and responding to texts* • Recognise usefulness of techniques such as visualisation, prediction, empathy in exploring the meaning of texts.

Scottish C for E objectives	NC assessment focuses	Comprehension skills	ICT Talk activities
Listening and Talking *Creating texts (fourth level)* Communicate in a clear and expressive manner and independently select and organise appropriate resources as required. ***Reading*** *Finding and using information (third and fourth levels)* Use the features of different types of text to find, select, sort, summarise, link and use information from different sources; make notes and organise them, explore issues and create new texts.	AF2, AF4	***Literal*** – finding information, summarising ***Inference*** – interpreting information, prediction ***Analysis*** – text structure ***Evaluation*** – social context	Object grid Question maker
Listening and Talking *Tools for listening and talking (third and fourth levels)* Can respond in ways appropriate to their role and use contributions to reflect on, clarify or adapt thinking; can explore and expand on contributions. ***Reading*** *Understanding, analysing and evaluating (third and fourth levels)* Can identify and discuss similarities and differences between different types of text and compare and contrast different types of text.	AF5, AF7	***Literal*** – finding information ***Clarification*** ***Inference*** – interpreting information ***Analysis*** – language use ***Evaluation*** – empathy	Story map Text formatter (playscript)
Listening and Talking *Tools for listening and talking (third level)* Make relevant contributions when engaging with others, encourage others to contribute and acknowledge that they have the right to hold a different opinion. ***Reading*** *Finding and using information (third and fourth levels)* Can make notes and organise them to explore issues and create new texts, using own words as appropriate.	AF3, AF7	***Literal*** – finding information ***Inference*** – interpreting information ***Clarification*** ***Evaluation*** – empathy, prediction ***Analysis*** – language use	Dilemma vote Question maker
Listening and Talking *Understanding, analysing and evaluating (third and fourth levels)* Develop an informed view through learning about the techniques used to influence opinion; learn how to assess the value of different sources. ***Reading*** *Understanding, analysing and evaluating (third and fourth levels)* Develop an informed view through learning about techniques used to influence opinion; learn to recognise persuasion and bias, and assess the reliability of information and the credibility and value of different sources.	AF5, AF6	***Literal*** – finding information ***Inference*** – interpreting information ***Clarification*** ***Analysis*** – language use, text structure ***Evaluation*** – author viewpoint	Information categoriser Text formatter (letter)
Listening and Talking *Finding and using information (third and fourth levels)* Can make notes and organise these to develop thinking, explore issues and create new texts, using own words as appropriate. ***Reading*** *Finding and using information (third and fourth levels)* Can make notes and organise them to develop thinking, retain and recall information, explore issues and create new texts, using own words as appropriate.	AF2, AF7	***Literal*** – finding information ***Inference*** – interpreting information ***Clarification*** ***Evaluation*** – empathy, historical context	Dilemma vote Text formatter (playscript)

Unit 1

Trouble for Oliver!

▸ Understanding the layout conventions of playscripts

Oliver asks for more

Characters:	Oliver Twist Mr Bumble, master of the workhouse Boy 1 Boy 2 Boy 3
Scene:	*The* ***workhouse.*** *A large hall at suppertime. The boys are seated at a long, wooden table. There is a bowl and spoon in front of each of them.*
MR BUMBLE:	Now, boys, let us thank the Good Lord for the food he has kindly given us.
	[The boys mumble ***grace without enthusiasm****. The* ***gruel*** *is served.]*
BOY 1:	*(whispering)* I tell you, if I don't get more food, I might just wake up one night and **devour** that skinny boy in the next bed!
BOY 2:	*(slopping a spoonful of gruel back into his bowl)* Look at this muck. Ain't worth eating. Fat old Bumble doesn't eat this muck!
BOY 3:	Well, it's all we get and we're going to have seconds! **It's sorted**. Oliver here is going to ask for more, ain't you Oliver?
OLIVER:	*(Oliver smiles weakly and eats as slowly as he can.)* Ye–es. When I've finished this. I have to finish this first.
BOY 3:	*(threateningly)* Well, be quick about it!
MR BUMBLE:	Have we all finished?
	[The boys whisper to each other and wink at Oliver.]
BOY 3:	*(giving Oliver a* ***vicious*** *poke)* Go on then. You drew the short straw. You've got to do it!
	[Oliver gets up from the table with his bowl and spoon. He walks towards Mr Bumble and stops in front of him.]
OLIVER:	Please, Sir, I want some more.
	[Mr Bumble turns pale. He looks in astonishment at Oliver.]
MR BUMBLE:	*(in a faint voice)* What?
OLIVER:	Please, Sir, I want some more.

Scene based on *Oliver Twist* by Charles Dickens

- How many characters are in the scene?
- Where is the scene set?
- How do you know who is speaking?
- Which brackets are used to tell the actors how to 'say' or 'do' something?
- Which brackets are used to 'tell the story'?
- Explain the meaning of the words and phrases in **bold**.
- Why do you think the boys said grace 'without enthusiasm'?
- How do you know Boy 1 is really hungry?
- How do you think Oliver feels when he walks up to Mr Bumble?
- How do you know that Mr Bumble is shocked by what Oliver says?

Extracts

Oliver asks for more
Oliver and the undertaker
Oliver meets the Artful Dodger
Scenes based on *Oliver Twist* by Charles Dickens

Planning

Dramatic conventions

Objectives

Renewed Primary Literacy Framework Year 5
3 *Group discussion and interaction*
- Understand different ways to take the lead and support others in groups.

4 *Drama*
- Perform a scripted scene making use of dramatic conventions.
- Use and recognise the impact of theatrical effects.

5 *Engaging with and responding to texts*
- Explore how writers use language for comic and dramatic effects.

Assessment focuses
AF2 Understand, describe, select or retrieve information, events or ideas from texts and use quotation and reference to text
L3 Include quotations from or references to text
L5 Make inferences and deductions based on evidence.
AF4 Identify and comment on the structure and organisation of texts
L3–L5 Identify an increasing number of organisational features at text level.

Scottish Curriculum for Excellence: Literacy
Listening and Talking
Understanding, analysing, evaluating (third level)
Shows understanding of what they listen to or watch by commenting, with evidence, on the content and form of short and extended texts.
Reading
Finding and using information (third/fourth levels)
Able to make notes and organise them to develop their thinking, help retain and recall information, explore issues and create new texts, using their own words as appropriate.

TEACH

In this unit the pupils will investigate and revise the conventions of playscripts as a springboard to using these conventions in a non-fiction context. 'Extra' activities and plenary sessions build on pupils' familiarity with the characters and setting in the scenes to enable them to create non-fiction media pieces.

Before reading

- What do pupils understand by the term 'workhouse'?
- Elicit / explain the concept of the workhouse in Victorian times.

Reading

- What do pupils know about the story *Oliver Twist*?
- The story so far: Oliver is an orphan. His mother died in the workhouse when he was born and Oliver, having nowhere else to go, grows up there.
- The extract can be read to the class by the teacher, by individuals in the class or individually.

After reading

Use the panel prompts in the Pupil Book as the basis of a class discussion.

ICT

- How many characters are in the scene?
  Five speaking: Oliver, Mr Bumble, Boy 1, Boy 2, Boy 3.
- Where is the scene set?
  In a large hall in the workhouse at suppertime.
- How do you know who is speaking?
  The character's name appears on the left of the page in capitals.
- Which brackets are used to tell the actors how to 'say' or 'do' something?
  Curved brackets, e.g. (whispering).
- Which brackets are used to 'tell the story'?
  Square brackets, e.g. [Oliver gets up from the table with his bowl and spoon].
- Explain the meaning of the words and phrases in bold:
  workhouse: *a place where poor people and orphans lived;* ***grace:*** *a prayer thanking God;* ***without enthusiasm:*** *with no interest / grudgingly;* ***gruel:*** *a thin soup of boiled grain;* ***devour:*** *eat very quickly;* ***It's sorted:*** *It has been taken care of;* ***vicious:*** *extremely violent.*
- Why do you think the boys said grace 'without enthusiasm'?
  Answers that suggest they knew the awful food they were getting – they saw little reason to say thank you!
- How do you know that Boy 1 is really hungry?
  He has been thinking of eating the boy in the next bed.
- How do you think Oliver is feeling when he walks up to Mr Bumble?
  Answers that suggest Oliver is frightened, probably wishing that somebody else had to do it.
- How do you know that Mr Bumble is shocked by what Oliver says?
  Answers that use the evidence of stage directions: [Mr Bumble turns pale. He looks in astonishment at Oliver.] (in a faint voice).

Oliver and the undertaker

After Oliver had dared to 'ask for more', the people who run the workhouse want rid of him. Mr Bumble takes him to be an apprentice to an undertaker.

Characters:	Oliver Twist Mr Bumble, master of the workhouse Mr Sowerberry, the undertaker Mrs Sowerberry, his wife
Scene:	*The undertaker's shop at dusk.*
	[Mr Sowerberry is making some entries in his day-book by the light of a dismal candle when Mr Bumble and Oliver arrive.]
MR SOWERBERRY:	Ah! Is that you, Bumble?
MR BUMBLE:	No one else, Mr Sowerberry. Here, *(pushing Oliver forward)* I've brought the boy.
	[Mr Sowerberry raises the candle above his head and peers at Oliver. Oliver makes a small bow.]
MR SOWERBERRY:	Oh, that's the boy, is it? *(He turns to the back of the shop.)* Mrs Sowerberry! Will you have the goodness to come here a moment, my dear?
	[Mrs Sowerberry comes from a room at the back of the shop.]
MR BUMBLE:	Good evening, Mrs Sowerberry.
	[She ignores Bumble and peers at Oliver. Oliver bows again.]
MR SOWERBERRY:	My dear, this is the boy from the workhouse that I told you of.
MRS SOWERBERRY:	Dear me, he's very small.
MR BUMBLE:	*(anxiously)* Why, he is rather small. There's no denying it. But he'll grow, Mrs Sowerberry, he'll grow…
MRS SOWERBERRY:	*(sharply)* Ah, I dare say he will on our victuals and our drink. I see no saving in parish children, not I. They always cost more to keep than they're worth. However, men always think they know best!
	[Mr Bumble hurriedly backs out of the door.]
MR SOWERBERRY:	*(fearfully)* Now my dear…
MRS SOWERBERRY:	There! Get downstairs, little bag o' bones.
	[Mrs Sowerberry opens a side door and pushes Oliver down a steep flight of stairs into a damp, dark stone cellar.]

Scene based on *Oliver Twist* by Charles Dickens

Understanding the scene

- Who are the characters in the scene?
- Where is the scene set?
- What is Mr Sowerberry doing when Mr Bumble and Oliver arrive?
- Pick out a stage direction that:
  a tells an actor/actress how to say the lines
  b tells an actor/actress what to do
  c relates the story.

Looking at words

Explain the meanings of these words as they are used in the scene:

a undertaker **b** dusk **c** dismal
d anxiously **e** sharply **f** victuals

Looking at character

- The scene is set 'at dusk'. The only light is 'a dismal candle'. How do you think the playwright wants the audience to feel?
- Why do you think Oliver has nothing to say in this scene?
- Why do you think Mr Bumble:
  a is anxious when Mrs Sowerberry says that Oliver is 'very small'?
  b leaves hurriedly?
- What impression do you get of Mrs Sowerberry?
- How do you think Oliver is feeling when he is pushed down the stairs to the cellar?

Extra

In the next part of the story, Oliver is:

- given some cold meat that has been saved for the dog
- taken back upstairs and told he is to sleep under the counter among the coffins.

Prepare and role-play the next scene of the play. It is set the following morning when Oliver is woken up by Mrs Sowerberry.

TEACH *continued ...*

 Plenary

- Ask for volunteers to be Oliver and Mr Bumble. The class act as interviewers and ask them questions about the incident in the extract.
- Make notes on the questions asked and the responses given on the board.
- Pupils then write up the 'interview', setting it out like a playscript.

TALK

 Before reading

- Explain that this scene shows what happens to Oliver after he asks for more – *he is taken to be an apprentice to an undertaker.*
- What do pupils understand by the term 'undertaker'?
- How would pupils feel about working at an undertaker's?

 Reading

Ask pupils to recap on the scene *Oliver asks for more*. The extract can be read to the class by the teacher, by individuals in the class or as a group.

 Discussion group

In groups, pupils discuss the questions and make notes on their responses. Ensure children understand that they do not always have to agree.

Understanding the scene

- Who are the characters in the scene?
  Oliver Twist / Mr Bumble, master of the workhouse / Mr Sowerberry, undertaker / Mrs Sowerberry, his wife.
- Where is the scene set?
  The undertaker's shop at dusk.
- What is Mr Sowerberry doing when Mr Bumble and Oliver arrive?
  'making some entries in a day book', i.e. writing / doing accounts, etc.
- Pick out a stage direction that:

  a tells an actor / actress how to say the lines
  'anxiously' / 'sharply' / 'fearfully'

  b tells an actor / actress what to do
  'pushing Oliver forward' / 'He turns to the back of the shop'

  c relates the story.
  'Mr Sowerberry is making some entries in his daybook by the light of a dismal candle when Mr Bumble and Oliver arrive.' / 'Mr Sowerberry raises the candle above his head and peers at Oliver. Oliver makes a small bow.' / 'Mrs Sowerberry comes from a room at the back of the shop.' / 'She ignores Bumble and peers at Oliver. Oliver bows again.' / 'Mr Bumble hurriedly backs out of the door.' / 'Mrs Sowerberry opens a side door and pushes Oliver down a steep flight of stairs into a damp, dark stone cellar.'

Looking at words

Explain the meanings of these words as they are used in the scene:
a ***undertaker:*** *someone whose job it is to make arrangements for funerals;* **b** ***dusk:*** *a period of time at the end of the day, just before it grows dark;* **c** ***dismal:*** *feeble / small and weak;* **d** ***anxiously:*** *in a worried voice / nervously;* **e** ***sharply:*** *unkindly / bitterly;* **f** ***victuals:*** *food*

Looking at character

- The scene is set 'at dusk'. The only light is 'a dismal candle'. How do you think the playwright wants the audience to feel?
  Answers that suggest the audience will feel sorry for Oliver going to this awful place. Maybe they will experience a little fear and apprehension – what is going to happen?
- Why do you think Oliver has nothing to say in this scene?
  Answers that suggest that either Oliver is too scared and unhappy to speak OR that, given the trouble he got into when he spoke out and 'asked for more' in the workhouse, he has decided it is better to say nothing!
- Why do you think Mr Bumble:

  a is anxious when Mrs Sowerberry says that Oliver is 'very small'?
  Answers that suggest Mr Bumble is very worried that Mrs Sowerberry won't take Oliver.

  b leaves hurriedly?
  Answers that suggest Mr Bumble doesn't want to give her the chance to refuse.
- What impression do you get of Mrs Sowerberry? **ICT**
  Answers that suggest she is a cruel, bitter woman who Mr Sowerberry is afraid of. She has no pity for Oliver.
- How do you think Oliver is feeling when he is pushed down the stairs to the cellar?
  Individual answers. Possibly he is fearful and unhappy OR there is some sense of relief that he has escaped from the workhouse.

Oliver meets the Artful Dodger

Oliver has a terrible time at the undertakers and he decides to run away to London. He arrives at the town of Barnet and stops to rest.

Characters: Oliver Twist
The Artful Dodger, a street urchin

Scene: *A street in Barnet*

[Oliver, tired and hungry, is sitting on a doorstep when a boy stops and stares at him.]

DODGER: What's up with you then?

OLIVER: *(beginning to cry)* I am very hungry and tired. I have walked a long way. I have been walking these seven days.

DODGER: Walking for seven days! Beak's after you, eh?

OLIVER: *(looking surprised)* Isn't a 'beak' a bird's mouth?

DODGER: *(laughing)* You don't know much, do you? The beak's the magistrate. And if you're running from the law, I'm your man!

[Oliver is about to protest, but Dodger is helping him up.]

DODGER You want grub and you shall have it!

[Dodger buys ham and bread at a nearby shop.]

OLIVER: *(eating ravenously)* Thank you, Sir, thank you.

DODGER: *(looking around all the time)* Going to London?

OLIVER: *(between mouthfuls)* Yes, I am.

DODGER: *(slyly)* Got any lodgings?

OLIVER: No.

DODGER: Money?

OLIVER: No. Do you live in London?

DODGER: Yes, when I'm at home. I suppose you need some place to sleep tonight?

OLIVER: *(earnestly)* I do indeed.

DODGER: Don't fret. I know a respectable old gentleman who'll give you lodgings for free. Eat up, and then I'll take you to meet Mr Fagin and the other lads.

Scene based on *Oliver Twist* by Charles Dickens

Understanding the scene

1 What is Oliver doing when he meets the Artful Dodger?
2 Why does the Dodger think Oliver is running away?
3 What does he give Oliver to eat?
4 Besides food, what does Oliver need?
5 Who is the Dodger going to take Oliver to meet?

Understanding the words

6 Explain the meaning of these words and phrases as they are used in the scene:

a artful	**b** urchin	**c** magistrate
d running from the law	**e** grub	**f** ravenously
g slyly	**h** earnestly	**i** respectable

Looking at character

7 What impression do you get of the Artful Dodger? What evidence is there that the Artful Dodger might not make a good friend for Oliver? Give evidence for your view.
8 How does Oliver react to the Dodger?
9 Why do you think Oliver is 'eating ravenously'?
10 Why do you think the Dodger is 'looking around' all the time he is questioning Oliver?

Extra

Script a radio interview with Oliver after he has met the Artful Dodger. Questions should be based on:

- where Oliver was and what he was doing
- how he feels about the Artful Dodger.

TALK *continued ...*

Extra

ICT

In the next part of the story, Oliver is:

- given some cold meat that has been saved for the dog
- taken back upstairs and told he is to sleep under the counter among the coffins.

Prepare and role-play the next scene of the play. It is set the following morning when Oliver is woken up by Mrs Sowerberry.

Ensure each member of the group contributes. The script should be prepared in note form before the pupils practise it.

Plenary

- Discuss pupils' ideas for the 'Extra' activity.
- Give time for group performances.

WRITE

Before reading

- What do pupils understand by the terms 'living on the street' / 'living rough'?
- How would they feel if they had to do this?

Reading

- Ask pupils to recap on Oliver's life so far. The extract can be read to the class by the teacher, by individuals in the class or individually.

Questions

Pupils answer the questions individually, drawing on their work in the previous class work (Teach) and group work (Talk).

Round-up

- Pupils can work in pairs and combine their ideas for the 'Extra' activity, choosing the best questions and responses from their individual work.
- In pairs, pupils can perform the radio interview.

Answer guidance

ICT

Understanding the scene

1 'Oliver ... is sitting on a doorstep.'
2 Dodger thinks he is 'running from the law'.
3 Ham and bread.
4 'some place to sleep tonight'.
5 'a respectable old gentleman'.

Understanding the words

6 **a artful:** crafty / deceitful; **b urchin:** raggedly dressed child usually living by his / her wits; **c magistrate:** an officer of the law; **d running from the law:** running away to avoid capture by the police; **e grub:** food; **f ravenously:** very hungrily; **g slyly:** craftily; **h earnestly:** seriously; **i respectable:** honest and decent.

Looking at character

7 Answers that suggest, in this scene, he comes across as helpful and kind. However, he may not be a good friend as he seems to know too much about running away from the law and could lead Oliver into trouble.
8 Answers that suggest Oliver is only too willing to take Dodger's help and is not at all suspicious.
9 Answers that suggest he probably hasn't eaten for a very long time.
10 Answers that suggest he is probably keeping an eye out for the police.

Extra

Individual answers.

Unit 2

Do adverts persuade you?

▸ Exploring the language of persuasion

The power of advertising

You're never alone with

Fastracks

Fashionable and funky

Fastracks will get you noticed

Everyone wants to know the trend-setter with the coolest heels in town!

Fastracks

Spend A Pound, Save A Life

Every year, hundreds of dogs are abandoned by their owners. Some are tied up miles from home. Some are thrown out of cars on motorways.

Poppy is just one of them.

Needydogs is a charity that saves these unwanted dogs, gives them a home and cares for them. But we can't do it without your help. Just £1 a month can save Poppy and other mistreated dogs from a lonely, horrible death. Please help by visiting our website:

www.needydogs.co.uk

Smoking Isn't Cool

Do you want to die of lung cancer?

Do you want your skin to age prematurely?

Do you want your gums to rot?

Smoking is addictive

Don't start and if you have, then stop!

- Look at each advertisement.
- What is its purpose?
- Who is the audience?
- Where would you expect to see it?
- Explain the meaning of these words: fashionable, funky, trend-setter, abandoned, mistreated, prematurely, addictive.
- What 'emotion' is each advertisement appealing to?
- How has each advertisement used persuasive language, illustration, fonts and colour?
- Which advertisement do you find the most persuasive? Explain your reasons.

Extracts

The power of advertising
The copywriter's job
Sail Away To The Holiday Of Your Dreams!

Planning

Persuasive writing

Objectives

Renewed Primary Literacy Framework Year 5

1 *Speaking*

- Present a spoken argument, sequencing points logically, defending views using persuasive language.

2 *Listening and responding*

- Analyse the use of persuasive language.

7 *Understanding and interpreting texts*

- Infer writers' perspectives from what is written and what is implied.
- Explore how writers use language for dramatic effects.

Assessment focuses

AF5 Explain and comment on writer's use of language, including grammatical features at word and sentence level
L3 Identify a few basic features of writer's use of language
L4 Comment and show some awareness of the effect of writer's language choices.

AF6 Identify and comment on writer's purposes and viewpoints, and the overall effect of the text on the reader
L3 Identify main purpose of writer
L4 Summarise a writer's viewpoint in simple terms
L5 Identify purpose and show awareness of writer's viewpoint and overall effect on the reader.

Scottish Curriculum for Excellence: Literacy

Listening and Talking
Understanding, analysing, evaluating (third level)
Develop an informed view through learning about the techniques used to influence opinion; learn how to assess the value of different sources, and recognise persuasion.

Reading
Understanding, analysing, evaluating (third level)
Develop an informed view through learning about techniques used to influence opinion; learn to recognise persuasion, and assess the reliability of information.

TEACH

This is the first of two units based on the use of persuasive language. In this unit, pupils will investigate the language of advertisements and how it is designed to persuade the reader.

Before reading

Discuss what the pupils understand by the term 'advertising'.

- What do they think of advertising – pros and cons.
- Which adverts do they like / dislike?
- Have they ever been persuaded to buy something or do something because of an advert?

Reading

- Explain that the pupils are going to look at three advertisements that are designed to persuade people to do different things.
- The texts can be read to the class by the teacher, by individuals in the class or individually.

After reading

Use the panel prompts in the Pupil Book as the basis of a class discussion.

- What is the purpose of each advertisement?
To persuade people to **a:** *buy Fastracks;*
b: *give money to save homeless dogs;* **c:** *give up smoking OR not to start smoking.*
- Who is the audience of each advertisement?
a: *young people;* **b:** *people who care about animals;*
c: *people who smoke / people who might begin to smoke.*
- Where would you expect to see each advertisement?
All adverts could be found in newspapers and magazines; **b:** *as a poster in a vet's surgery;* **c:** *as a poster in a doctor's surgery.*
- Explain the meaning of these words:
fashionable: *dressed in a way that is popular at this time;* ***funky:*** *fashionable in a way that is unusual and shows a lot of imagination;* ***trend-setter:*** *wear something new (i.e. Fastracks) that becomes popular;* ***abandoned:*** *left;* ***mistreated:*** *treated badly;* ***prematurely:*** *before it should do naturally;* ***addictive:*** *something that you want more and more and cannot do without.*
- What 'emotion' is each advertisement appealing to?
Answers that suggest **a:** *the need to be popular, someone who is looked up to / the fear of being alone, unpopular;* **b:** *feelings of pity and the 'warm' feeling that comes from doing good;* **c:** *feelings of fear*
- How has each advertisement used persuasive language, illustration, fonts and colour?
Individual answers.
- Which advertisement do you find the most persuasive? Explain your reasons.
Individual answers.

Plenary

- Discuss 'real' adverts that the pupils know.
- Can they identify how they are being persuaded and what emotion the adverts are appealing to?

The copywriter's job

When we look at an advertisement, we see the finished article. But it begins as an idea that a copywriter has to turn into a successful advert.

Style Sheet 1: Rough layout

Advert for: Fun City Theme Park
Size: A4 – handout
Rough layout

Background – blurred photo of big wheel in theme park?
Title – name of theme park
Photograph of entrance? Main attraction?
Blurb – description? quotes? persuasive words & phrases?
Information – opening times/ price/café/other facilities/ directions?

Style Sheet 2: Adding detail to the layout

Title – blocked caps – colour?
Red / yellow? Heavy black outline?
Illustration – photograph – include people – happy – enjoying themselves
Blurb – possible adjectives amazing incredible thrilling scary
black text
persuasive phrases value for money breathtakingly exciting a must
blue text
Info – opening times 9am to sunset / 364 days a year
café light lunch to three course meal
prices Adults £10 / children £4 / family ticket for four £25
Also – disabled access
Find us at (check motorway routes)

Understanding the style sheets

- What is the advertisement for?
- How will people see the advertisement?
- Find two examples of words or phrases used to persuade.
- Find two examples of information.
- What will a group of two adults and two children save by buying a family ticket?

Looking at words

Explain the meaning of these words and phrases as they are used on the style sheets:

a main attraction **b** blurb **c** facilities
d breathtakingly exciting **e** disabled access **f** motorway routes

Exploring further

- Why do you think Style Sheet 1 includes a 'rough layout'?
- Why do you think some items on the style sheets are followed by a question mark and others are not?
- Who do you think the quotes would be from in the blurb?
- Explain what you think the difference between the 'Blurb' and the 'Info' is.
- What do you think happens after the style sheets are finished?

Extra

Using the style sheets and your own ideas, produce an advertisement for Fun City Theme Park.

TALK

Before reading

- What do pupils understand by the term 'copywriter'? Explain, if necessary, that a copywriter writes the text for advertisements.
- Do they think it would be an interesting job? Why? Why not?

Reading

- Explain to the children that they are going to look at some ideas a copywriter has for advertising *Fun City Theme Park*.
- The extract can be read to the class by the teacher, by individuals in the class or as a group.

Discussion group

In groups, pupils discuss the questions and make notes on their responses. Ensure pupils understand that they do not always have to agree.

Understanding the style sheets

- What is the advertisement for?
  Fun City Theme Park.
- How will people see the advertisement?
  As a handout.
- Find two examples of words or phrases used to persuade.
  Any two of: amazing / incredible / thrilling / scary / value for money / breathtakingly exciting / a must / family ticket.
- Find two examples of information.
  Any two of: opening times / price / other facilities / directions.
- What will a group of two adults and two children save by buying a family ticket?
  £3

Looking at words

Explain the meaning of these words and phrases as they are used on the style sheets:

a *main attraction:* *the one that attracts the most people to come and see it / use it;* **b *blurb:*** *writing that is designed to persuade people;* **c *facilities:*** *things for people to use;* **d *breathtakingly exciting:*** *so amazing it takes your breath away;* **e disabled access:** *ways of getting into and around the theme park for people in wheelchairs;* **f *motorway routes:*** *ways you can get to the theme park using the motorways.*

Exploring further

- Why do you think Style Sheet 1 includes a 'rough layout'?
  Answers that suggest it is to give people an idea of what the finished advertisement will look like.
- Why do you think some items on the style sheets are followed by a question mark and others are not?
  Answers that suggest that those followed by a question mark are just 'ideas' at this point whereas those not followed by a question mark have been decided on.
- Who do you think the quotes would be from in the blurb?
  Answers that suggest from people who run the theme park / satisfied customers of the theme park.
- Explain what you think the difference between the 'Blurb' and the 'Info' is. ICT
  Answers that suggest the 'Blurb' is written to persuade; the 'Info' gives factual details.
- What do you think happens after the style sheets are finished?
  Encourage groups not simply to come up with 'they make the advert'. Prompt them to think of possible stages, e.g. final decisions on wording / font size; artwork / photographs to be chosen; final layout to be decided.

Extra

- Using the style sheets and your own ideas, produce an advertisement for Fun City Theme Park. ICT

Plenary

ICT

- Discuss finished adverts for the 'Extra' activity. Choose the most persuasive by a class vote. Voters should be able to give reasons.

25 nights from £2,000

Sail Away To The Holiday Of Your Dreams!

This is the chance of a lifetime with prices starting at only £2,000.

Cabin Grade	Price
Inside twin	£2,000
Outside twin	£2,500
Superior outside twin	£2,999
Balcony cabin	£3,400
Balcony suite	£3,999

This is an amazing opportunity to sail in luxury around the sun-drenched islands of the Caribbean on board the world-class *Olympia*.

You will stay in elegant, spacious cabins; enjoy sumptuous meals; and be entertained by world-famous cabaret artists.

Some days will be spent exploring the beautiful, unspoilt islands of St Lucia, Antigua and Barbados. On other days, you can relax aboard and enjoy all that the *Olympia* has to offer as we cruise gently in the crystal waters of the Caribbean.

Places are limited, so book without delay!
Phone 0845 000 000
Visit our website: www.crystalsail.com

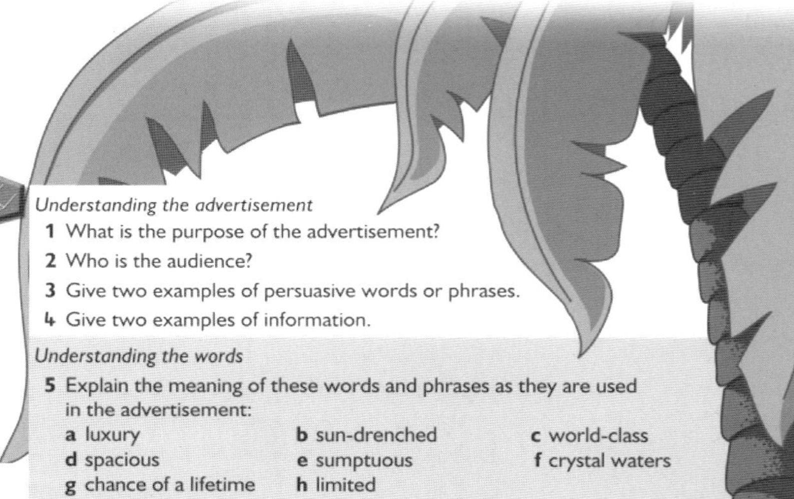

Understanding the advertisement

1 What is the purpose of the advertisement?
2 Who is the audience?
3 Give two examples of persuasive words or phrases.
4 Give two examples of information.

Understanding the words

5 Explain the meaning of these words and phrases as they are used in the advertisement:
a luxury **b** sun-drenched **c** world-class
d spacious **e** sumptuous **f** crystal waters
g chance of a lifetime **h** limited

Exploring the advertisement

6 Why do you think the advertisement begins with:
a the cheapest price **b** a photograph of the cruise ship?
7 Look at the words 'luxury', 'elegant' and 'sumptuous'. Why do you think the writer uses these words?
8 What does the writer mean when he says the islands are 'unspoilt'?
9 Why do you think people would pay more for an 'outside twin cabin' than an 'inside twin cabin'?
10 Does the advertisement persuade you that this would be 'The Holiday Of Your Dreams'? Why? Why not?

Extra

Imagine that you are thinking of booking the cruise on the *Olympia* but you want more information. Make a list of questions you will ask when you make the phone call.

WRITE

Before reading

Discuss holiday advertisements with the pupils.

- What do they usually look like / tell you?
- What do pupils understand by the term 'cruise'?
- Can they say where the Caribbean is?

Reading

- Explain to the children that they are going to look at an advertisement for a Caribbean cruise. Then read the advertisement.
- The advertisement can be read to the class by the teacher, by individuals in the class or individually.

Questions

Pupils answer the questions individually, drawing on their work in the previous class work (Teach) and group work (Talk).

Round-up

- Use children's ideas for the 'Extra' activity as a basis for a class discussion.
- Recap on what pupils have learned about persuasive writing in advertisements.

Answer guidance

Understanding the advertisement

1 To persuade people to book a cruise on the *Olympia.*
2 Adults who are fairly well-off.
3 Examples such as: the heading / 'amazing opportunity' / 'sun-drenched islands' / 'world-class' / 'elegant, spacious cabins' and so on.
4 Examples such as: the price / islands that will be visited / telephone number / web site.

Understanding the words

5 **a luxury**: expensive and high quality surroundings; **b sun-drenched**: bathed in sunlight: **c world-class**: one of the best in the world; **d spacious**: very roomy; **e sumptuous**: impressive / expensive; **f crystal waters**: clear, sparkling water; **g chance of a lifetime**: something that only comes along once in a lifetime; **h limited**: there are only so many places on board.

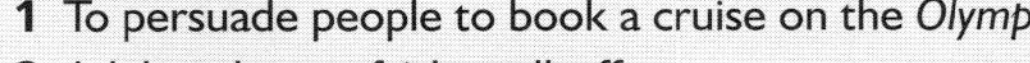

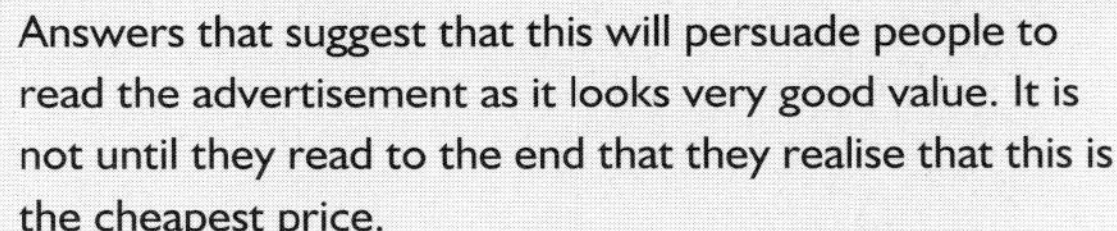

Exploring the advertisement

6 **a** Answers that suggest that this will persuade people to read the advertisement as it looks very good value. It is not until they read to the end that they realise that this is the cheapest price.
b Answers that suggest the photograph will make a visual impression on the reader. They will be persuaded to read on because of how wonderful it looks.
7 Answers that recognise that these words are persuasive.
8 Answers that suggest the islands are not overrun with tourists / they have not been changed in a way that makes them less beautiful and not worth visiting.
9 Answers that suggest an outside cabin will have a view of the ocean.
10 Individual answers.

Extra

Individual answers.

Meeting Great-Aunt Dymphna

The Gareth children – Alex, Penny, Robin and Naomi – are sent to stay with their Great-Aunt Dymphna in Ireland. Their first meeting with their Great-Aunt is an alarming experience! They soon realise that they will have to fend for themselves during their stay.

The first impression of Great-Aunt Dymphna was that she was more like an enormous bird than a great-aunt. This was partly because she wore a black cape, which seemed to flap behind her when she moved. Then her nose stuck out of her thin wrinkled old face just like a very hooked beak. On her head she wore a man's tweed hat beneath which straggled wispy white hair. She wore under the cape a shapeless long black dress. On her feet, despite of it being a fine warm evening, were rubber boots.

The children gazed at their great-aunt, so startled by her appearance that the polite greetings they would have made **vanished** from their minds. Naomi was so scared that, though tears went on rolling down her cheeks, she did not make any more noise. Great-Aunt Dymphna had turned her attention to the luggage.

'**Clutter**, clutter! I could never abide clutter. What have you got in all this?' As she said 'this' a rubber boot kicked at the nearest suitcase.

'Clothes, mostly,' said Alex.

'Mummy didn't know what we'd need,' Penny explained, 'so she said we'd have to bring everything.'

'Well, as it's here we must take it home I suppose,' said Great-Aunt Dymphna. 'Bring it to the car,' and she turned and, like a great black eagle, swept out…

'She's as mad as a coot,' Alex whispered to Penny. 'I should think she ought to be in an asylum.'

Penny shivered. 'I do hope other people live close to Reenmore. I don't like us to be alone with her.'

But in Bantry where they stopped to send a **cable** nobody seemed to think Great-Aunt Dymphna mad. It is true the children understood very little of what was said, for they were not used to the Irish **brogue**, but it was clear from the tone of voice used and the expressions on people's faces that what the people of Bantry felt was respect. It came from the man who filled the car up with petrol, and another who put some parcels in the boot.

'Extraordinary!' Alex whispered to Penny when he came out of the hotel. 'When I said "Miss Gareth said it would be all right to send a cable" you'd have thought I said the Queen has said it was all right.'

'Why, what did they say?' Penny asked.

'It was more the way they said it than what they said, but they told me to write down the message and they would telephone it through right away.'

It was beginning to get dark when they left Bantry but as the children peered out of the windows they could just see the purplish mountains, and that the roads had fuchsia hedges instead of ordinary bushes, and that there must be ponds or lakes for often they caught the shimmer of water.

'At least it's awfully pretty,' Penny whispered to Alex. 'Like Mummy said it would be.'

'I can't see how that'll help if she's mad,' Alex whispered back.

Suddenly, without a word of warning, Great-Aunt Dymphna stopped the car.

'We're home.' Then she chuckled. 'I expect you poor little town types thought we'd never make it, but we always do. You'll learn.'

The children stared out of the car windows. Home! They seemed to be in a lonely lane miles from anywhere.

'Get out. Get out,' said Great-Aunt Dymphna. 'There's no drive to the house. It's across that field.'

'Horrible old beast!' thought Alex, dragging their cases from the boot. 'She really is **insufferable**.' But he kept what he felt to himself for out loud all he said was, 'Let's just take the cases we need tonight. We can fetch the others in the morning.'

Alex led the way, carrying his and Naomi's cases. Robin came next. Penny, gripping Naomi's hand, followed the boys. 'I don't wonder nobody brings a telegram here,' said Robin. 'I shouldn't think anybody brings anything. I should think we could all be dead before a doctor comes.'

Alex could have hit him.

From *The Growing Summer*, Noel Streatfeild

- Who are the characters in the story?
- Where does this part of the story take place?
- What does Great-Aunt Dymphna look like?
- What do the **bold** words mean as they are used in the story?
- The children find themselves in a difficult situation: What impression do you get of each of the children? How do they react to Dymphna?
- How do other people react to Dymphna?
- How do you think the author wants you to feel about her?
- How do you feel about her?

Extracts

The Growing Summer Noel Streatfeild
The Wolves of Willoughby Chase Joan Aiken
Ash Road Ivan Southall

Planning

Stories by significant authors

Objectives

Renewed Primary Literacy Framework Year 5
7 *Understanding and interpreting texts*
- Infer writer's perspectives from what is written and what is implied.
- Explore how writers use language for comic and dramatic effects.

Assessment focuses
AF3 Deduce, infer and interpret information, events and ideas from texts
L3 Begin to explain own interpretations of characters and motives using the text
L4 Show understanding of character and motives through explanation and prediction
L5 Use full range of evidence to comment on characters and motives.

AF6 Identify and comment on writer's purposes and viewpoints, and the overall effect of the text on the reader
L3 Identify main purpose of writer
L4 Identify purpose and show awareness of writer's viewpoint and overall effect on the reader
L5 Clearly identify purpose and viewpoint, and be aware of and explain the effect on reader.

Scottish Curriculum for Excellence: Literacy
Listening and Talking
Tools for listening and talking (third level)
Make relevant contributions when engaging with others, encourage others to contribute and acknowledge that they have the right to hold a different opinion.
Reading
Enjoyment and choice (third and fourth levels)
Give reasons, with evidence, for their personal responses.

TEACH

In this unit, pupils will read extracts from stories by long-established children's authors. The extracts concentrate on character portrayal, allowing pupils to investigate how authors create characters and manipulate reader response through description, dialogue and actions.

Before reading

- Discuss what pupils understand by the term 'characters' in stories.
- Discuss how readers get to know a character through author description (appearance, personality); by what a character says and does; by how a character relates to other characters.
- Ask pupils to give examples of favourite characters from their own reading and say why they like them.

Reading

- Explain to pupils they are going to read an extract from a story called *The Growing Summer.*
- The story so far: The Gareth children – Alex, Penny, Robin and Naomi – are sent to stay with their Great-Aunt Dymphna in Ireland. They very much have to fend for themselves during their stay and they find the first meeting with their Great-Aunt an alarming experience.
- The extract can be read to the class by the teacher, by individuals in the class or individually.

After reading

ICT

Use the panel prompts in the Pupil Book as the basis of a class discussion.

- Who are the characters in the story?
  Great Aunt Dymphna, Alex, Penny, Robin and Naomi.
- Where does this part of the story take place?
  There are multiple settings: first they are loading and getting into a car; then they stop at Bantry; finally they stop in a field near Dymphna's home.
- What does Great-Aunt Dymphna look like?
  Encourage pupils to use quotes about her physical appearance from the text, e.g. 'like an enormous black bird' / 'wore a black cape' / 'thin wrinkled face' / nose 'like a very hooked beak'.
- What do the bold words mean as they are used in the story?
  vanished: *disappeared;* ***clutter:*** *lots of things, usually untidy and unnecessary;* **cable:** *telegram;* **brogue:** *accent;* ***insufferable:*** *unbearable.*
- The children find themselves in a difficult situation. What impression do you get of each of the children?
  Answers based on evidence: Alex – considerate / realises the difficult situation but doesn't want to upset the others by speaking out loud; Penny – slightly nervous about the situation / tries to make the best of it; Robin – outspoken / doesn't necessarily think before he speaks; Naomi – frightened and upset.
- How do they react to Dymphna?
  Answers based on evidence: Alex thinks she is 'as mad as a coot'; Penny is very wary – 'I don't like us to be alone with her'; Robin thinks she is so odd that nobody would ever visit her; Naomi is very scared.

Miss Slighcarp

Miss Slighcarp is governess to Bonnie and her orphaned cousin Sylvia. When Bonnie's parents go away, and Miss Slighcarp is left in charge, the children soon find out she is no ordinary governess! This part of the story takes place in the schoolroom.

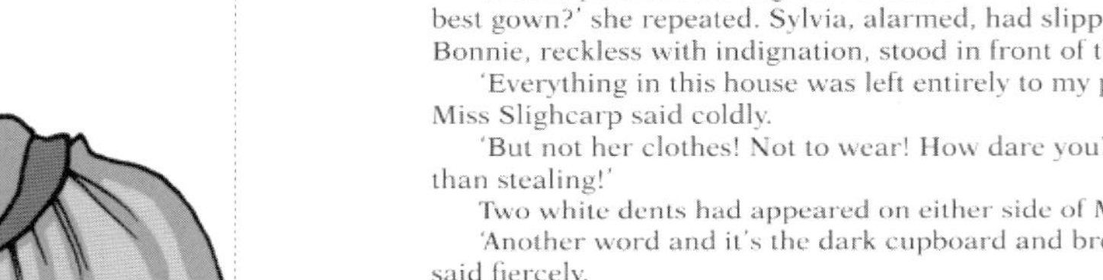

The governess, who had been examining some books on the shelves, swung round with equal abruptness. She seemed astonished to see them.

'Where have you been?' she demanded angrily, after an instant's pause.

'Why,' Sylvia faltered, 'merely in the next room, Miss Slighcarp.'

But Bonnie, with choking utterance, demanded, 'Why are you wearing my mother's dress?'

Sylvia had observed that Miss Slighcarp had on a draped gown of old gold velvet with ruby buttons, far grander than the grey twill she had worn the day before.

'Don't speak to me in that way, miss!' retorted Miss Slighcarp in a rage. 'You have been spoiled all your life, but we shall soon see who is going to be mistress now. Go to your place and sit down. Do not speak until you are spoken to.'

Bonnie paid not the slightest attention. 'Who said you could wear my mother's best gown?' she repeated. Sylvia, alarmed, had slipped into her place at the table, but Bonnie, reckless with indignation, stood in front of the governess, glaring at her.

'Everything in this house was left entirely to my personal disposition,' Miss Slighcarp said coldly.

'But not her clothes! Not to wear! How dare you? Take it off at once! It's no better than stealing!'

Two white dents had appeared on either side of Miss Slighcarp's nostrils.

'Another word and it's the dark cupboard and bread-and-water for you, miss,' she said fiercely.

'I don't care what you say!' Bonnie stamped her foot. 'Take off my mother's dress!'

Miss Slighcarp boxed Bonnie's ears. Bonnie seized Miss Slighcarp's wrists. In the confusion a bottle of ink was knocked off the table, spilling a long blue trail down the gold velvet skirt. Miss Slighcarp uttered an exclamation of fury.

'Insolent, ungovernable child! You shall suffer for this!' With iron strength she thrust Bonnie into a closet containing crayons, globes and exercise books, and turned the key on her. Then she swept from the room.

Sylvia remained seated, aghast, for half a second. Then she ran to the cupboard door – but alas! Miss Slighcarp had taken the key with her.

From *The Wolves of Willoughby Chase*, Joan Aiken

Understanding the passage

- Who are the characters in the story?
- What has Miss Slighcarp done to make Bonnie so angry?
- What happens to the dress and what does Miss Slighcarp then do to Bonnie?
- Explain the meaning of these words as they are used in the extract:

a abruptness	**b** astonished	**c** utterance
d observed	**e** retorted	**f** reckless
g disposition	**h** insolent	**i** aghast

Looking at character

- What impressions do you get of Bonnie, Sylvia and Miss Slighcarp?
- If you had been in this situation, would you have acted like Bonnie or Sylvia? Give your reasons.

Extra

Choose one of the group to be Miss Slighcarp. The rest of the group question her about the incident with the dress. She wants to appear reasonable and to get you on her side. What questions will you ask? What responses will she give?

TEACH *continued ...*

- How do other people react to Dymphna?
  Answers that suggest other people act with great respect towards her, and the children find that puzzling.
- How do you think the author wants you to feel about her?
  Discuss the feelings she might evoke. Would pupils find her scary / comic? Ask them to explain why.
- How do you feel about her?
  Individual answers.

Plenary

Discuss how pupils have found out about the various characters. Ensure pupils understand not only to look at what the author tells them, but also to examine what characters say and do in order to build up a picture of personality.

TALK

Before reading

- What do pupils understand by the term 'governess'?
- What do they think are the advantages / disadvantages of having a governess and being taught at home, as opposed to going to school?
- Have they read other stories where there is a governess?

Reading

- Explain to pupils they are going to read an extract from a story called *The Wolves of Willoughby Chase*. The story is set in 1832 when wolves roamed the countryside in the north of England. Sylvia is an orphan who comes to stay with her cousin Bonnie. One day, Bonnie's parents go away in a ship and Miss Slighcarp, an evil woman, arrives to look after the children. Her aim is to get rid of them but Bonnie and Sylvia are not going quietly!
- The extract can be read to the class by the teacher, by individuals in the class or in groups.

Discussion group

In groups, pupils discuss the questions and make notes on their responses. Ensure pupils understand that they do not always have to agree.

Understanding the passage

- Who are the characters in the story?
  Miss Slighcarp, Bonnie, Sylvia.
- What has Miss Slighcarp done to make Bonnie so angry?
  She is wearing Bonnie's mother's best gown.
- What happens to the dress and what does Miss Slighcarp then do to Bonnie?
  Ink is spilled on the dress. Miss Slighcarp then boxes Bonnie's ears and locks her in a cupboard.
- Explain the meaning of these words as they are used in the extract:
  a ***abruptness:*** *suddenness;* **b** ***astonished:*** *very surprised;* **c** ***utterance:*** *something spoken;* **d** ***observed:*** *noticed;* **e** ***retorted:*** *replied angrily;* **f** ***reckless:*** *not thinking about the consequences;* **g** ***disposition:*** *the power to do as one wants with something;* **h** ***insolent:*** *offensive / arrogant / insulting;* **i** ***aghast:*** *horrified.*

Looking at character

ICT

- What impressions do you get of Bonnie, Sylvia and Miss Slighcarp?
  Answers based on evidence:
  Bonnie: *The braver of the two girls. She confronts Miss Slighcarp, 'Why are you wearing my mother's dress?' She does not do as she is told, 'Bonnie paid not the slightest attention.' She stands her ground, 'Take off my mother's dress!'*
  Sylvia: *The more timid of the two girls. She does as she is told, 'Sylvia, alarmed, had slipped into her place at the table …'; she does nothing while Miss Slighcarp is in the room. 'Sylvia remained seated …'*
  Miss Slighcarp: *She expects to be obeyed, 'Don't speak to me that way, miss!' / 'Do not speak until you are spoken to'. She is cruel and violent: 'Miss Slighcarp boxed Bonnie's ears.' / 'thrust Bonnie into a closet'.*
- If you had been in this situation, would you have acted like Bonnie or Sylvia? Give your reasons.
  Encourage all members of the group to contribute.

Extra

ICT

Choose one of the group to be Miss Slighcarp. The rest of the group question her about the incident with the dress. She wants to appear reasonable and get you on her side. What questions will you ask? What responses will she give?
Ask for a group to volunteer to stage the interview for the rest of the class. The other groups can add questions that they would like to ask.

Plenary

- Ask pupils how they made their judgements about the characters.
- Do they think Sylvia was more or less sensible that Bonnie in the circumstances?

Bush Fire!

The story begins late one Friday evening, when three boys are camping in the Australian bush. The weather is very hot and there is a dry north wind. In the middle of the night, Wallace wakes up to find Graham making coffee. Accidentally, Graham knocks over a bottle of methylated spirits, which catches fire.

'It's burning,' howled Graham.

A blue flame snaked from the little heater up through the rocks towards the bottle in the boy's hand; or at least that was how it seemed to happen. It happened so swiftly it may have deceived the eye. Instinctively, to protect himself, Graham threw the bottle away. There was a shower of fire from its neck, as from the nozzle of a hose.

'Oh my gosh,' yelled Wallace and tore off his sleeping-bag. 'Harry!' he screamed. 'Wake up, Harry!'

They tried to stamp on the fire, but their feet were bare and they couldn't find their shoes. They tried to smother it with their sleeping-bags, but it seemed to be everywhere. Harry couldn't even escape from his bag; he couldn't find the zip fastener, and for a few awful moments in his confusion between sleep and wakefulness he thought he was in his bed at home and the house had burst into flames around him. He couldn't come to grips with the situation; he knew only dismay and the wildest kind of alarm. Graham and Wallace, panicking, were throwing themselves from place to place, almost sobbing, beating futilely at the widening arc of fire. Every desperate blow they made seemed to fan the fire, to scatter it farther, to feed it.

'Put it out,' shouted Graham. 'Put it out.'

It wasn't dark any longer. It was a flickering world of tree trunks and twisted boughs, of scrub and saplings and stones, of shouts and wind and smoke and frantic fear. It was so quick. It was terrible.

'Put it out,' cried Graham, and Harry fought out of his sleeping-bag, knowing somehow that they'd never get it out by beating at it, that they'd have to get water up from the creek. But all they had was a four-pint billy-can.

The fire was getting away from them in all directions, crackling through the scrub down-wind, burning fiercely back into the wind. Even the ground was burning: grass, roots and fallen leaves were burning, humus was burning. There were flames on the trees, bark was burning, foliage was flaring, flaring like a whip-crack; and the heat was savage and searing and awful to breathe.

'We can't, we can't,' cried Wallace. 'What are we going to do?'

'Oh, gee,' sobbed Graham. He was crying and he hadn't cried since he was twelve years old. 'What have I done? *We've got to get it out!*'

Harry was scrambling around wildly, bundling all their things together. It was not just that he was more level-headed than the others; it was just that he could see the end more clearly, the hopelessness of it, the absolute certainty of it, the imminent danger of encirclement, the possibility that they might be burnt alive. He could see all this because he hadn't been in it at the start. He wasn't responsible; he hadn't done it; and now he was wide awake he could see more clearly. He screamed at them, 'Grab your stuff and run for it.' But they didn't hear him or didn't want to hear him. They were blackened, their feet were cut, even their hair was singed. They beat and beat, and the fire was leaping into the tree-tops, and there were no black shadows left, only bright light, red light, yellow light, light that was hard and cruel and terrifying, and there was a rushing sound, a roaring sound, explosions, and smoke, smoke like a hot red fog.

'No,' cried Graham. 'No, no, no.' His arms dropped to his sides and he shook with sobs and Wallace dragged him away. 'Oh, Wally,' he sobbed. 'What have I done?'

'We've got to get out of here,' shouted Harry. 'Grab the things and run.'

'Our shoes!' cried Wallace. 'Where are they?'

'I don't know. I don't know.'

'We've got to find our shoes.'

'They'll kill us,' sobbed Graham. 'They'll kill us. It's a terrible thing, an awful thing to have done.'

'Where'd we put our shoes?' Wallace was running around in circles, blindly. He didn't really know what he was doing. Everything had happened so quickly, so suddenly.

'For Pete's sake run!' shouted Harry.

From *Ash Road*, Ivan Southall

Understanding the passage

1 Who are the characters in the story?
2 What are they doing?
3 At first, how did they try to put out the fire?
4 When Harry woke up, what did he think had happened?
5 What was it that Harry knew they needed to put out the fire?

Looking at words

6 Explain the meaning of these words and phrases as they are used in the extract:
a instinctively **b** futilely **c** encirclement
d deceived the eye **e** come to grips with

Looking at character

7 Who is thinking more clearly when the fire starts: Graham or Wallace? Find evidence to support your view.
8 Find evidence in the passage that Graham and Wallace panic as the fire spreads. Think about: what the author tells us; what the boys do and say.
9 Graham says, 'We've got to get it out.' Harry says, 'We've got to get out of here.' How is each boy reacting to the situation? Explain in your own words why Graham and Harry are reacting so differently.

Extra

Choose one of the characters in the passage and retell the incident from his point of view. Remember to include your character's thoughts and feelings as well as what happened.

WRITE

Before reading

- What do pupils understand by 'a bush fire'?
- Where do bush fires happen?
- Why are they so dangerous?
- Have they seen pictures on television or in magazines that show raging bush fires? How did they feel when they looked at these pictures?

Reading

- Explain to pupils they are going to read an extract from a story called *Ash Road*.
- The extract can be read to the class by the teacher, by individuals in the class or individually.

Questions

Pupils answer the questions individually, drawing on their work in the previous class work (Teach) and group work (Talk).

Round-up

- Use the three extracts as a basis for a class discussion to investigate how pupils made judgements about the characters.

Answer guidance

Understanding the passage

1 Wallace (Wally), Graham, Harry.
2 They are camping in the Australian bush.
3 'They tried to stamp on the fire...' / 'They tried to smother it with their sleeping bags…'
4 Harry thought he was at home and the house was on fire.
5 Harry knew that they needed water.

Looking at words

6 **a instinctively:** without thinking; **b futiley:** uselessly; **c encirclement:** being surrounded; **d deceived the eye:** made them think they had seen something that had not actually happened; **e come to grips with:** fully realise what was happening.

Looking at character

7 Answers that suggest Graham is not thinking clearly as he throws the burning bottle away from him, and that Wallace is thinking clearly enough at this point to wake up Harry.
8 Graham and Wallace panic.
- what the author tells us: 'Graham and Wallace panicking…'; Graham – 'He was crying…'
- what the boys do: 'throwing themselves from place to place…'; ' beating futilely…'; 'running around in circles…'
- what the boys say: 'Put it out.'; 'What are we going to do?'; What have I done?'; 'They'll kill us.'

9 Graham's words show that he is only thinking of trying to put right what he has done.
Harry's words show that he is thinking ahead. He realises that they are never going to put the fire out and they should concentrate on their own safety.
Graham and Harry react so differently because of how the fire started. Graham is responsible for the fire and he wants to put it right. Harry is not responsible for what has happened. The situation was already out of control when he woke up. This means he is not feeling guilty, as Graham is, so 'he can see more clearly' and understands that there is nothing they can do but save themselves.

Extra

Ensure pupils understand that they must not just copy the description from the extract but put themselves in the character's situation and really think of how they would be feeling, not only about the fire but also the way in which the others behave.

How to use Booksbooks – your online bookshop

Task: Find and buy *The Secret Garden* by Frances Hodgson Burnett.

Instructions

1 Go to the hyperlink http://www.booksbooks.co.uk. This will bring up the Homepage with a list of **options**.

2 Double click on 'Books'.

3 On the Books page, look at the list of **categories**.

4 Double click on 'Children's Books'.

5 Look at the top of the Children's Books page. You will see:

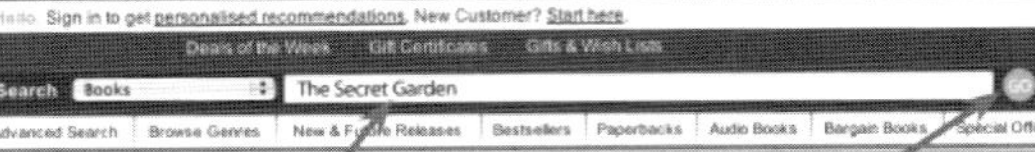

6 Type *The Secret Garden* here:

7 Click on GO.

8 This page will show you all the different **editions** and prices.

9 Click on the edition that you want to buy.

10 This page will give you details of the book you have **selected**.

11 If you want to buy it, click on BUY NOW.

- What is Booksbooks?
- What does it sell?
- Which category does *The Secret Garden* come under?
- If you bought the selected book, how much would you pay?
- Explain the meaning of the words in **bold** as they are used on the web page.
- Explain why you think the instructions:
  - are numbered
  - are written in short, simple sentences
  - include diagrams.
- Do you think these instructions are easy to follow or not? Explain your reasons.
- Compare shopping for a book in a bookshop with shopping for a book online. List the advantages and disadvantages of both.

Extracts

How to use Booksbooks – your online bookshop
How to download photographs to your desktop
Alarm clock

Planning

Instructions

Objectives

Renewed Primary Literacy Framework Year 5

7 *Understanding and interpreting texts*
- Compare different types of information texts and identify how they are structured.

8 *Engaging with and responding to texts*
- Compare the usefulness of techniques such as visualisation.

9 *Creating and shaping texts*
- Create multi-layered texts, including use of hyperlinks, linked with web pages.

Assessment focuses

AF4 Identify and comment on the structure and organisation of texts, including grammatical and presentational features at text level

L3/L4 and **L5** Identify increasing numbers of features, with increasing comment and explanation.

AF5 Explain and comment on writer's use of language, including grammatical features at word and sentence level

L3/L4 Identify basic features of writer's use of language, with simple comments on choices

L5 Show some awareness of the effect of the writer's language choices.

Scottish Curriculum for Excellence: Literacy

Listening and Talking

Finding and using information (third level)

Can identify and give an accurate account of the purpose of the text, identify and discuss similarities between different types of text and use this information.

Reading

Finding and using information (third and fourth levels)

Can use knowledge of features of different types of text to find, select, sort, summarise, link and use information from different sources.

TEACH

In this unit the pupils will investigate instructional writing in the context of their own ICT use. Each set of instructions has clear examples of the features of this text type.

Before reading

- What can pupils remember about the features of instructional writing? i.e. imperative verbs; present tense; numbered / short simple sentences, supported by diagrams.
- What do they use the web for?
- Have they (their family) ever bought anything on the web?

Reading

- Explain to pupils they are going to read a set of instructions for buying a book from an online bookshop.
- The text can be read to the class by the teacher, by individuals in the class or individually.

After reading

Use the panel prompts in the Pupil Book as the basis of a class discussion.

ICT

- What is Booksbooks?
  An online bookshop.
- What does it sell?
  Books; audio books; DVDs; PC and video games; computer software.
- Which category does *The Secret Garden* come under? *Books*
- If you bought the selected book, how much would you pay?
  £7.49 (including postage and packing).
- Explain the meaning of the words in bold as they are used on the web page:
  options: *choices;* ***categories:*** *groups of things that are similar;* ***editions:*** *copies of the book that are published at different times;* ***selected:*** *chosen.*
- Explain why you think the instructions:
  - are numbered
  To show the order in which they must be followed.
  - are written in short, simple sentences
  To make them easy to understand.
  - include diagrams
  To help the reader see what the screen should look like at each stage of the instruction.
- Do you think these instructions are easy to follow or not? Explain your reasons.
  Individual answers.
- Compare shopping for a book in a bookshop with shopping for a book online. List the advantages and disadvantages of both.
  Advantages online: carry bigger stock / often cheaper / usually offer both new and second hand editions
  Advantages bookshop: if book in stock, you can have it immediately / you can browse and handle books
  Disadvantages online: have to pay postage & packing / have to wait for book to be delivered
  Disadvantages bookshop: if not in stock, book has to be ordered / often more expensive.

How to download photographs to your desktop

You will need:

- a PC
- a digital camera memory card
- a USB card reader.

Instructions

1 Switch on the computer.

2 Plug the USB CARD READER into the USB PORT.

3 Place the digital camera MEMORY CARD into the card reader.

4 Select OPEN FOLDER TO VIEW FILES.

5 Press OK.

6 Select DCIM FOLDER (Digital Camera images).

7 Select the folder containing the photograph you want to download.

8 Select the photograph.

9 Select COPY 2 icon.

10 Select DESKTOP icon.

11 Press SAVE.

Your photograph is now saved on your desktop.

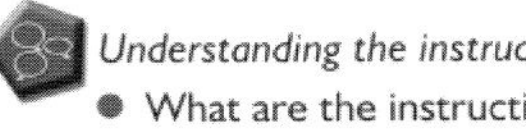

Understanding the instructions

- What are the instructions for?
- How many instructions are there?
- What equipment do you need?
- What is on the USB card reader?

Looking at words

Explain the meaning of these words as they are used in the instructions:

a port **b** select **c** download **d** icon **e** desktop

Exploring further

- Make a list of the features of instructional writing that you can find in these instructions.
- If someone had not downloaded photographs before, do you think these instructions would be easy or difficult to follow? Explain your reasons.
- Once you have stored your photographs on your computer, what could you do to share them with other people?

Extra

Photographs can be printed and kept in albums, or kept or stored on a computer. Discuss and list the advantages and disadvantages of both these methods of storing photographs.

TEACH *continued ...*

Plenary

- Discuss what is easy to sell online and what is more difficult.

TALK

Before reading

- Ask pupils where they (their family) store their photographs.

Reading

- Explain to pupils they are going to read a set of instructions for downloading photographs and storing them on a computer.
- The extract can be read to the class by the teacher, by individuals in the class or as a group.

Discussion group

In groups, pupils discuss the questions and make notes on their responses. Ensure pupils understand that they do not always have to agree.

Understanding the instructions

- What are the instructions for?
  Downloading photographs from your digital camera to your desktop.
- How many instructions are there? *11*
- What equipment do you need?
  A PC; a digital camera memory card; a USB card reader.
- What is on the USB card reader?
  The photographs you have taken.

Looking at words

Explain the meaning of these words as they are used in the instructions:

a ***port:*** *connection;* **b** ***select:*** *choose;* **c** ***download:*** *to move information to your computer from another source;* **d** ***icon:*** *a small picture on a computer that stands for a function;* **e** ***desktop:*** *the screen that shows the files stored on the computer.*

Exploring further

- Make a list of the features of instructional writing that you can find in these instructions.
  Answers should include: numbers; short, simple sentences; diagrams; imperative verbs; present tense.
- If someone had not downloaded photographs before, do you think these instructions would be easy or difficult to follow? Explain your reasons. ICT
  Individual answers.
- Once you have stored your photographs on your computer, what could you do to share them with other people?
  Individual answers, e.g. print; enlarge; crop; send via e-mail.

Extra ICT

Photographs can be printed and kept in albums or kept or stored on a computer. List the advantages and disadvantages of both these methods of storing photographs.

Individual answers, e.g. cost; space for storage; ability to copy; ability to look at them away from a computer. Ensure all members of the group contribute ideas.

Plenary

Use groups' answers to the last question in 'Exploring further' and the 'Extra' activity as a basis for a class discussion.

Alarm clock

Most mobile phones can be set like an alarm clock.

Instructions to set the alarm

1

Unlock your phone by pressing the SELECT KEY followed by the HASH KEY.

2

Use the SELECT KEY to get into MENU.

3

On the MENU screen, scroll down using the DIRECTION KEY and choose ORGANISER.

4

On the ORGANISER screen, scroll down using the DIRECTION KEY and choose ALARM CLOCK.

5

Switch the alarm on by using the left or right DIRECTION KEY.

6

Use the bottom DIRECTION KEY to scroll down to the alarm time.

7

Use the NUMBER KEYS to enter the time you want the alarm to go off.

8

Press the CLOSE KEY and you will be asked 'SAVE CHANGES?'

9

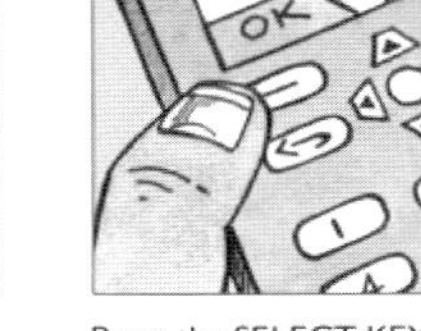

Press the SELECT KEY and 'ALARM SAVED' will appear.

Understanding the instructions

1 What are the instructions for?

2 How many instructions are there?

3 What key do you use to scroll down the MENU screen?

4 What keys do you use to set the time?

Understanding the words

5 Explain the meaning of these words and phrases as they are used in the instructions:

a hash key **b** menu **c** scroll down

Exploring further

6 Why do you think the intructions are numbered?

7 Why do you think the instructions include diagrams?

8 Why do you think some words are in capitals?

9 Think of at least three reasons why you might want to set an alarm on your mobile phone.

10 Do you think these instructions are easy to follow or not? Explain your reasons.

Extra

Think of a piece of equipment you use at home or at school.
Write a set of simple instructions for one of its functions.

Before reading

- How many pupils have a mobile phone?
- Do pupils think they are a good idea? Why? Why not?
- What can they do besides make phone calls?
- What do pupils mainly use their mobile phone for?

Reading

- Explain to pupils that they are going to read a set of instructions about setting an alarm clock on a mobile phone.
- The instructions can be read to the class by the teacher, by individuals in the class or individually.

Questions

Pupils answer the questions individually, drawing on their work in the previous class work (Teach) and group work (Talk).

Round-up

- Go over the features of instructional writing, e.g. numbered instructions, short simple sentences, use of diagrams, imperative verbs.

Answer guidance

Understanding the instructions

1 Setting an alarm on a mobile phone.
2 Nine.
3 Direction key.
4 Number keys.

Understanding the words

5 **a hash key**: key marked with the hash sign #; **b menu**: a selection of things to choose from; **c scroll down**: move down the screen.

Exploring further

6 To show the order in which they must be followed.
7 To help the reader see what should be on the screen at each stage.
8 Answers that suggest the important 'technical' words are in capitals.
9 Individual answers, suggesting things like to help owner to get up in the morning, or to follow a recipe with oven times, or a reminder to do something.
10 Individual answers, pupils may suggest no – too many technical terms are confusing, or yes, the words and diagrams are very clearly linked and illustrated, so not confusing.

Extra

Individual answers.

Unit 5

Heroes and villains

▸ **Understanding the roles of heroes and heroines**

Teach

The Sword and the Stone

When the service was over they all **passed out of** the church and went into the churchyard, where they beheld a wonderful sight.

A great square stone lay there, and in the stone was an **anvil**, and through anvil and stone was a sword. About the sword were written in letters of gold these words: 'He who pulleth this sword out of this stone and anvil is the rightly born King of England.'

When all the lords saw these words they tried, one after another, to pull the sword out of the stone. But no one was able to move it from its place. 'He is not here,' said the Archbishop, 'who can draw out the sword. I do not doubt, however, but God will make him known. Let us **appoint** ten knights, men of good fame, to keep watch over the sword.'

Then they agreed among themselves to meet on a future day, and to let any man who wished try his skill at withdrawing the sword. The Archbishop arranged that on New Year's Day there should be a **tournament**, and other fine doings, that the lords and commons should be kept together till the King should be revealed.

So upon New Year's Day the lords came together; and among them rode Sir Ector, a noble knight and one who had loved King Uther well, and in his company his son Sir Kay (who had received his knighthood but last Hallowmass), and young Arthur, his adopted son, who was but a youth.

As they rode to the place of meeting, Sir Kay found that he had left his sword behind at their lodging, and he asked young Arthur to ride back and bring it for him.

'Right gladly will I do that,' said the boy. 'Haste you on with our father. I will return to the town with all speed and will bring your sword.'

When he reached their lodging he knocked hard at the door, but no one answered, for they had all gone to the tournament.

Arthur was angry, and said to himself: 'I will ride to the churchyard and take the sword from the stone, for I do not wish my brother to be without a sword this day.'

When he came to the churchyard he **alighted** from his horse, and, going to the anvil, lightly pulled the sword out of the stone; and, mounting his horse again, he rode as fast as he could back to Sir Kay and gave him the sword.

Sir Kay grasped the sword, well pleased. **His eye ran down it**, and he knew it was the sword from the stone. He hastened to rejoin his father and tell him the news.

'Sir,' cried he, when he came up to Sir Ector, 'surely I, and none other, am chosen to be King of England, since in my hand I bear the sword of the stone!'

Sir Ector led his son and the boy Arthur into the church, and commanded his son to tell him truly how he had got the sword.

Sir Kay's **face fell**, but he answered stoutly:

'My brother Arthur brought it to me.'

Then said Sir Ector to Arthur, 'Tell me, did you **pluck** the sword from the stone?'

Arthur at once confessed how, when he had reached home, he had found no one in the house to give him his brother's sword, so he had made all haste to the churchyard and plucked the sword from the stone that rested there.

'Were none there,' asked Sir Ector, 'to **forbid** the act?'

'Nay,' said the boy, 'they had gone, every one, to the tournament.'

This was true, for the knights had gone to try their skill.

Then said Sir Ector to Arthur: 'I know well you must be King of the land.'

'Wherefore should I be King?' asked Arthur.

'Sir,' was Ector's reply, 'it is clearly **ordained**. For the man who can draw the sword out of the stone shall be rightful King of this land.'

From *King Arthur and His Knights*, anonymous

- What was in the churchyard?
- What was going to happen on New Year's Day?
- What do we know about Arthur?
- Why did Arthur pull the sword from the stone?
- What do the **bold** words and phrases mean as they are used in the extract?
- Why do you think all the Lords tried to pull the sword from the stone?
- What impression do you get of Arthur and Sir Kay?
- Arthur was Sir Ector's 'adopted' son. Who do you think Arthur's real father might have been?
- Do you think Arthur will be a 'hero' or a 'villain' in the rest of the story?

Extracts

King Arthur and His Knights Anonymous
Krishna and Kaliya
The Storm Eric and Tessa Hadley

Planning

Traditional stories, fables, myths and legends

Objectives

Renewed Primary Literacy Framework Year 5
3 *Group discussion and interaction*
- Plan and manage a group task over time using different levels of planning.

4 *Drama*
- Reflect on how working in role helps to explore complex issues.

7 *Understanding and interpreting texts*
- Use evidence from across a text to explain events.

8 *Engaging with and responding to texts*
- Use techniques such as visualisation, prediction and empathy in exploring the meaning of texts.

Assessment focuses
AF3 Deduce, infer or interpret information, events or ideas from texts
L3/L4 Identify relevant points, with increasing use of comments, quotations and textual reference
L5 Develop explanation of inferred meanings, drawing from evidence across the text.
AF7 Relate texts to social, cultural and historical traditions
L3/L4 Make connections between texts; recognise and make simple comments on context
L4/L5 Recognise similarities and differences between texts; explain how context links to a text's meaning.

Scottish Curriculum for Excellence: Literacy
Listening and Talking
Creating texts (third level)
Develop confidence when engaging with others, and communicate in a clear and expressive way
Reading
Understanding, analysing and evaluating (third/fourth levels)
Identify and discuss similarities and differences between texts, and compare and contrast different texts.

TEACH

In this unit, pupils will investigate myths and legends from around the world in which heroic deeds are performed against frightening villains, and lives are risked to help others.

Before reading

- What do pupils understand by the terms 'myth' and 'legend'?
- What myths / legends do they know already?
- What do they know about King Arthur?

Reading

- Explain that pupils are going to read an extract from *King Arthur and His Knights*. The king, Uther Pendragon, has died after a long illness. But who will now be king?
- The extract can be read out by the teacher, by individuals in the class or individually.

After reading

Use the panel prompts in the Pupil Book as the basis of a class discussion.

ICT

- What was in the churchyard?
  'A wonderful sight' / 'a great grey stone' / 'in the stone was an anvil' / 'through the anvil and the stone was a sword' / 'letters of gold: He who pulleth this sword out of this stone and anvil is rightly King of England.'
- What was going to happen on New Year's Day?
  'a tournament, and other fine doings' where 'any man who wished' could 'try his skill at withdrawing the sword'.
- What do we know about Arthur?
  He was the adopted son of Sir Ector; brother to Sir Kay; 'rightful King of this land'.
- Why did Arthur pull the sword from the stone?
  He did it so that his brother would have a sword for the tournament. Encourage pupils to explain the causal sequence of events leading to this.
- What do the bold words and phrases mean as they are used in the extract?
  passed out of: *came out of;* ***anvil:*** *metal block on which a blacksmith shapes objects such as horseshoes;* ***appoint:*** *choose someone to do a particular job;* ***tournament:*** *a gathering where games or sports are played;* ***alighted:*** *got down / dismounted;* ***his eye ran down it:*** *he looked at it;* ***face fell:*** *he looked disappointed;* ***pluck:*** *take something quickly and easily;* ***forbid:*** *to say it wasn't allowed;* ***ordained****: officially ordered.*
- Why do you think all the Lords tried to pull the sword from the stone?
  Answers that suggest each one of the Lords wanted to be King.
- What impression do you get of Arthur and Sir Kay?
  Arthur – helpful (goes back for Kay's sword); thoughtful (doesn't want Kay to be without sword); loyal (doesn't contradict Sir Kay); truthful (confesses to pulling the sword from the stone).
  Sir Kay – ambitious (wants to be King); not entirely honest (implies he pulled the sword from the stone).
- Arthur was Sir Ector's 'adopted' son. Who do you think Arthur's real father might have been?
  Pupils should pick up that Sir Ector 'had loved King Uther well' and that Arthur could pull the sword from the stone to deduce King Uther was Arthur's real father.
- Do you think Arthur will be a 'hero' or a 'villain' in the rest of the story?
  Individual answers suggesting 'hero'.

Krishna and Kaliya

Krishna is a Hindu god, and legend has it that he was brought up in a cowherd's family. There are many myths about him. In this story, he defeats the Serpent King.

Krishna and his friends loved to play by the Yamuna river. On long summer days, while the cows were grazing close by, Krishna and the other boys would play throwing and catching a ball, tossing it high in the air and leaping strenuously to make sure it did not fall in the water.

For in the water was great danger. This stretch of the river was home to a serpent. Kaliya was an evil serpent that had many heads and could breathe terrible fire.

One day, while the boys were playing, Krishna climbed up a tree that hung over the riverbank. 'Throw the ball to me,' he cried.

One of his friends called out, 'Be careful! You are too close to the water!'

'Throw me the ball,' Krishna repeated.

One of the other boys tossed up the ball. Krishna leaned out from the tree but the ball slipped from his grasp and fell into the river.

The boys groaned in dismay but Krishna did not hesitate. He leaped in the river to retrieve the ball. The other boys watched fearfully. For a moment there was complete silence, then a deafening roar came from the water as Kaliya rose up. Its many terrible heads thrashed about and fire and smoke poured from its many mouths.

The cows bolted in panic and the boys sprang back, shrieking and crying, so great was their fear. 'Where is Krishna?' one of them cried.

'He must surely be dead,' wailed another. 'The serpent has killed him!'

But Krishna was not dead. Kaliya had wrapped his body around the young boy but Krishna fought back and began attacking each of the serpent's heads in turn. He could make himself as heavy as the whole world and with this weight he danced on the heads of the serpent.

Kaliya's heads began to die one by one. The serpent realised that Krishna was no ordinary boy and that he could not defeat him. When he had no strength left, Kaliya became still, awaiting certain death.

But Krishna was merciful as well as strong. He knew that it was the nature of a serpent to be violent so he stopped his destructive dance and pardoned the creature. He banished him from the river and Kaliya slunk away, grateful to have escaped with his life.

Understanding the story

- What did Krishna and his friends do on 'long summer days'?
- What was extraordinary about Kaliya?
- Where did Kaliya live?
- Why did Krishna leap into the river?
- How did Krishna defeat the serpent?

Looking at words

Explain the meanings of these words and phrases as they are used in the story:

a strenuously **b** grasp **c** dismay **d** retrieve **e** bolted
f awaiting **g** merciful **h** destructive **i** banished

Exploring further

- What impression do you get of: **a** Krishna **b** Kaliya?
- When the ball fell into the water, why do you think the boys 'groaned in dismay'?
- Why did the serpent realise that Krishna was 'no ordinary boy'?
- Explain in your own words why Krishna spared the serpent's life.
- What makes Krishna the 'hero' of the story?

Extra

Discuss other stories, films or TV programmes you know where the hero/heroine defeats an evil monster.

Why do you think stories like this are so popular?

TEACH *continued …*

 Plenary

- Discuss the idea of 'heroes' and 'villains'.
- What characteristics does each character type have?
- Does Arthur have the characteristics of a hero?

TALK

Before reading

- What do the pupils know about the Hindu god Krishna? (Creator of the world; plays a flute; represented as a beautiful youth with bluish skin, wearing a crown of peacock feathers.)

 Reading

- Explain to pupils they are going to read a legend about the early life of Krishna.
- The legend can be read to the class by the teacher, by individuals in the class or as a group.

 Discussion group

In groups, pupils discuss the questions and make notes on their responses. Ensure pupils understand that they do not always have to agree.

Understanding the story

- What did Krishna and his friends do on 'long summer days'?
  They played ball by the Yamuna River.
- What was extraordinary about Kaliya?
  He had many heads and could breathe fire.
- Where did Kaliya live?
  He lived under the water in the Yamuna River.
- Why did Krishna leap into the river?
  Krishna leaped into the river to retrieve the ball which he had let fall into the water.
- How did Krishna defeat the serpent?
  Krishna made himself 'as heavy as the whole world' and used his weight to dance on and kill each of the serpent's heads in turn.

Looking at words

Explain the meaning of these words and phrases as they are used in the story:

a ***strenuously:*** *with a lot of effort;* b ***grasp:*** *very tight hold;* c ***dismay:*** *worry or fear;* d ***retrieve:*** *to go and get something back;* e ***bolted:*** *ran away in fear;* f ***awaiting:*** *expecting;* g ***merciful:*** *showing kindness from a position of power;* h ***destructive:*** *violent and aggressive;* i ***banished:*** *sent away for good.*

Exploring further

- What impression do you get of:

  a Krishna
  adventurous / quick thinking / resourceful / brave / strong / merciful

  b Kaliya?
  fierce / unfeeling / cruel / dangerous / powerful
- When the ball fell into the water, why do you think the boys 'groaned in dismay'?
  Answers that suggest that they thought the ball was lost because Kaliya was in the water.
- Why did the serpent realise that Krishna was 'no ordinary boy'?
  The serpent realised when Krishna fought back and made himself as heavy as the world to kill his heads.
- Explain in your own words why Krishna spared the serpent's life.
  Answers that suggest that Krishna realised the serpent was violent and evil by nature and deserved to be pardoned.
- What makes Krishna the 'hero' of the story?
  Individual answers.

 Extra

ICT

- Discuss other stories, films or TV programmes you know where the hero / heroine defeats an evil monster.
  Individual answers.
- Why do you think stories like this are so popular?
  Individual answers.

 Plenary

- Discuss what pupils have learned about heroes and villains so far, e.g. their characteristics, actions, etc.

The Storm

Once a rich mandarin was saved from a fierce storm at sea by a light that guided him to the safety of an island. The people of the island told him that the light was the lantern of the Lin maiden. This is the sad story the people of the island told the mandarin.

'…Hundreds of years ago, on the shore of the eastern sea, there lived a fisher family named Lin: a father, a mother, two sons, and a daughter – and such a daughter, known and loved along the whole coast. She was up first every morning to make breakfast for her parents. Then down to the sea with her father and brothers to help prepare the boats and nets. Every morning as they launched their boats against the incoming waves they heard her call, "Good wind and good weather!"

'Sir, you're beginning to dream by that warm fire, and perhaps it's the storm which fills your mind. That's how it was with the Lin maiden. She had been working with her mother one day. They'd had their midday meal and as she sat she began to feel sleepy, and she dreamed a strange dream.

'She dreamed of the five dragon brothers who live beneath the sea. Something had made them angry – and when they are angry, they lash their mile-long tails, mountains collapse into the sea and waves touch the sky.

'The fierce storm raged in her dream, and there, tossed about in their little boats, she saw her father and her brothers. She rushed to the seashore and waded into the water, and somehow she caught hold of the rope fastened to the bows of her father's boat. Holding this rope in her teeth she seized the ropes tied to her brothers' boats and began to pull them all to safety.

'Just then, her mother tried to wake her. "Daughter! Daughter!"

'The Lin maiden opened her mouth to answer, and in her dream the rope slipped from between her teeth and her father's boat disappeared under the waves.

'All through the afternoon, far into the evening, mother and daughter sat waiting, for what they knew must come. Only two brothers returned. "Our father's boat has been lost. He has gone to the Sea Dragon's Palace."

'The Lin maiden said nothing. She ran past her brothers and out of the house, down to the seashore; and there she plunged into the water to seek for her lost father…

'They never found the body, sir. But her brothers and other sailors started to see her out at sea, in the fiercest storms. No sailor who sees her is ever lost. They come safely to shore, as you did tonight, sir, with the help of her lantern.'

'The Storm' from *Legends of Earth, Air, Fire and Water* by Eric and Tessa Hadley

Understanding the story

1 What did the Lin maiden do every morning?

2 What did the five dragon brothers do when they were angry?

3 In her dream, how did the Lin maiden hold on to the ropes of her father's boat and her brothers' boats?

4 What happened when her mother woke her up?

5 When she realised her father was lost, what did the Lin maiden do?

Looking at words

6 Explain the meaning of these words as they are used in the story:

a launched **b** lash **c** collapse
d seized **e** plunged **f** lantern

Looking at character

7 What impression do you get of the Lin maiden?

8 Why do you think she called out, 'Good wind and good weather' when the boats were launched?

9 How do you think the dream made her feel?

10 How do you think she and her mother felt as they waited 'through the afternoon and far into the evening'?

11 Do you think the Lin maiden is the heroine of the story? Explain your reasons.

Extra

The mother and daughter waited all afternoon and evening for the men to come back. What do you think they said to each other? Write their conversation.

WRITE

Before reading

- Ask pupils if they know stories of heroines who saved people at the risk of their own life, e.g. Grace Darling.
- Do they think it is easy or difficult to risk your own life to help others? Encourage them to explain their reasons.

Reading

- Explain to pupils they are going to read a legend called 'The Storm' in which the spirit of a young girl helps people in trouble at sea.
- The extract can be read to the class by the teacher, by individuals in the class or individually.

Questions

Pupils answer the questions individually, drawing on their work in the previous class work (Teach) and group work (Talk).

Round-up

- Discuss the three 'heroes' in this unit. In what ways are they similar? In what ways are they different?

Answer guidance

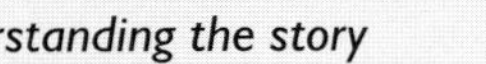

ICT

Understanding the story

1 She made 'breakfast for her parents' and then went 'down to the sea with her father and brothers to help prepare the boats and nets'.

2 '…when they are angry, they lash their mile-long tails'.

3 She held the rope attached to her father's boat 'in her teeth' and the ropes attached to her brothers' boats in her hands.

4 She opened her mouth and 'in her dream the rope slipped from between her teeth and her father's boat disappeared under the waves'.

5 'She ran past her brothers and out of the house, down to the seashore; and there she plunged into the water to seek for her lost father'.

Looking at words

6 **a launched**: got the boats onto the water; **b lash**: fling about with great force; **c collapse**: fall down; **d seized**: grabbed; **e plunged**: dived; **f lantern**: a light inside a glass container with a handle for carrying it.

Looking at character

7 Answers that are based on evidence: respectful / hard working: made breakfast and helped her father and brothers; very caring: grief-stricken when father was lost; very hard on herself: thought it was her fault that her father died; impulsive: plunged into the sea.

8 Answers that suggest she was wishing her father and brothers would have a good day's fishing and come home safely.

9 Answers that suggest she would have been frightened and worried by the dream, as she obviously believed it was telling her something.

10 Answers that suggest they would be anxious / worried / impatient.

11 Individual answers. Some may suggest she was not 'heroic' because she plunged into the waves and drowned herself; others may argue she had exceptional gifts and, after her death, still tried to help those in danger.

Extra

Individual answers.

An Egyptian Treasure!

GREAT FIND AT THEBES, LORD CARNARVON'S LONG QUEST.

From Our Cairo Correspondent, Valley of the Kings (by runner to Luxor), Nov 29.

This afternoon Lord Carnarvon and Mr Howard Carter **revealed** to a large company what promises to be the most **sensational** Egyptological discovery of the century.

The find consists of, among other objects, the funeral **paraphernalia** of the Egyptian King Tutankhamen, one of the famous **heretic** kings of the Eighteenth Dynasty.

The remarkable discovery announced to-day is the reward of patience, perseverance and **perspicacity**. For nearly sixteen years Lord Carnarvon, with the assistance of Mr Howard Carter, has been carrying out **excavations** on the part of the site of ancient Thebes situated on the west bank of the Nile at Luxor. Seven years ago work was started in the Valley of the Kings, after other excavators had abandoned the Valley. The search was continued systematically, and at last the dogged perseverance of Mr Carter, his thoroughness, above all his *flair*, were rewarded by the discovery. Mr Carter covered up the site and telegraphed to Lord Carnarvon, who at once came out from England.

The sealed outer door was carefully opened: then a way was cleared down some sixteen steps along a passage of about 25ft. The door to the chamber was found to be sealed as the outer door had been. With difficulty an entrance was effected, and when the last the excavators managed to squeeze their way in an extraordinary sight met their eyes, one that they could **scarcely credit**.

THE TREASURE WITHIN

First they saw three magnificent State couches, all gilt, with exquisite carving. On these rested beds, beautifully carved, gilt, inlaid with ivory and semi-precious stones and also innumerable boxes of exquisite workmanship. One of these boxes was inlaid with ebony and ivory, with gilt inscriptions; another contained **emblems** of the underworld; on a third, which contained Royal robes, handsomely embroidered, precious stones, and golden sandals, were beautifully painted hunting scenes.

There was a stool of ebony inlaid with ivory, with the most delicately carved duck's feet: also a child's stool of fine workmanship. Beneath one of the couches was the State Throne of King Tutankhamen, probably one of the most beautiful objects of art ever discovered. There was also a heavily gilt chair, with portraits of the King and Queen, the whole encrusted with turquoise, carnelian, lapis and other semi-precious stones.

Two life-sized bituminised statues of the King, with gold work holding a golden stick and mace, faced each other, the handsome features, the feet, and the hands delicately carved, with eyes of glass and head-dress richly studded with gems.

There were also four chariots, the sides of which were encrusted with semi-precious stones and rich gold decoration. These were dismantled, with a charioteer's apron of leopard skin hanging over the seat.

- Where would you expect to find an article like this?
- What is the article about?
- Name three things that were found in the tomb.
- Explain the meanings of the **bold** words and phrases as they are used in the article.
- Would the headline make you want to read the article? Why? Why not?
- What impression do you get of Howard Carter?
- Why do you think 'other excavators had abandoned the Valley'?
- Why do you think the chariots had been 'dismantled'?
- There are eight paragraphs in the article. Say briefly what each is about.

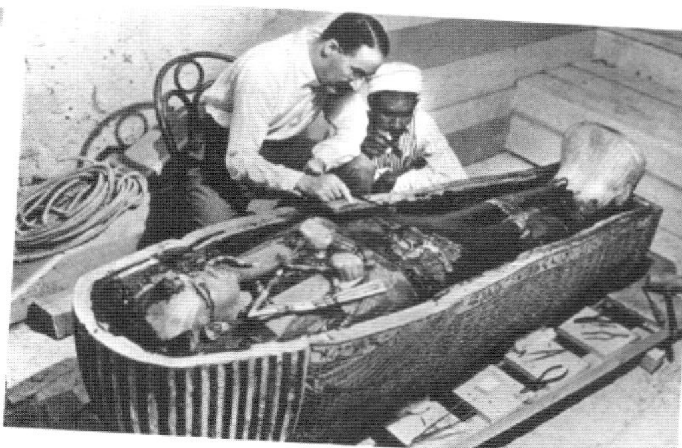

Extracts

An Egyptian Treasure!
Treasures of the past
The Valley of the Kings

Planning

Exploring the use of recount in the media

Objectives

Renewed Primary Literacy Framework Year 5

3 *Group discussion and interaction*

- Plan and manage a group task over time using different levels of planning.
- Understand different ways to take the lead and support others in groups.

7 *Understanding and interpreting texts*

- Use evidence from across a text to explain events.

Assessment focuses

AF2 Understand, describe, select or retrieve information, events or ideas from texts and use quotation and reference to text

L3 Include quotations from or references to text
L4 Make inferences based on evidence in the text
L5 Make inferences and deductions based on textual evidence.

AF4 Identify and comment on the structure and organisation of texts, including presentational features at text level

L3–L5 Identify an increasing number of organisational features at text level.

Scottish Curriculum for Excellence: Literacy

Listening and Talking

Creating texts (fourth level)

Communicate in a clear and expressive manner and independently select and organise appropriate resources as required.

Reading

Finding and using information (third/fourth levels)

Use the features of different types of text to find, select, sort, summarise, link and use information from different sources; make notes and organise them, explore issues and create new texts.

TEACH

In this unit pupils will investigate recount texts in the context of the media. The articles are connected by the theme of Tutankhamen and include activities such as charting chronology, devising questions and research.

 Before reading

- What do pupils understand by the term 'archaeology'?
- What do pupils know about Tutankhamen / Tutankhamun?
- Examine these words: Egypt, Egyptology, Egyptological.

 Reading

- Explain that Howard Carter was the archaeologist who discovered the tomb of King Tutankhamen. The money for the excavation came from Lord Carnarvon.
- Pupils are going to read part of a newspaper report that was written only days after Carter made his discovery in the 1920s.
- The extract can be read to the class by the teacher, by individuals in the class or individually.

 After reading

Use the panel prompts in the Pupil Book as the basis of a class discussion.

ICT

- Where would you expect to find an article like this? *A newspaper.*
- What is the article about?
  The discovery of Tutankhamen's tomb by Howard Carter.
- Name three things that were found in the tomb.
  Any three of: state couches / beds / boxes / royal robes / precious stones / golden sandals / a stool / a child's stool / state throne / gilt chair / two life-size statues / four chariots / charioteer's apron.
- Explain the meanings of the bold words and phrases as they are used in the article.
  revealed: *showed;* ***sensational:*** *exciting and surprising;* ***paraphernalia:*** *various objects;* ***heretic:*** *someone who does not believe in a place's official religion;* ***perspicacity:*** *the ability to judge a situation quickly and correctly;* ***excavations:*** *the process of digging in the ground to find things from the past;* ***scarcely credit:*** *find it difficult to believe;* ***emblems:*** *symbols.*
- Would the headline make you want to read the article? Why? Why not? *Individual answers.*
- What impression do you get of Howard Carter?
  Answers based on evidence – 'reward of patience, perseverance and perspicacity' / 'The search was continued systematically' / 'dogged perseverance' / 'his thoroughness, above all his flair'.
- Why do you think 'other excavators had abandoned the valley'?
  Answers suggesting that the excavators may have run out of patience, money or ideas, or thought there was nothing left to find in the valley.
- Why do you think the chariots had been 'dismantled'?
  Answers that suggest they were too big to get into the tomb in one piece, based on the evidence: 'when the last of the excavators managed to squeeze their way in'.

Treasures of the past

This is a transcript of a radio programme where the interviewer, Fiona Jacobs, talks to an expert in archaeology.

Fiona Jacobs: Good evening. I'm Fiona Jacobs and you are listening to Treasures of the Past, a series of programmes that looks at astounding archaeological discoveries. Tonight, I'm joined by Professor Simon Black, an expert on Ancient Egypt, and we'll be discussing the discovery of Tutankhamen's tomb. Good evening, Professor Black.

Simon Black: Good evening.

Fiona Jacobs: Most people know about the amazing treasures Howard Carter found in the first chamber of the tomb, but why was he so sure there was a second chamber?

Simon Black: Well, as Carter says in his biography, among all the treasures 'there was no coffin or trace of a mummy'. So they looked for and found another sealed doorway between two life-sized figures of the King.

Fiona Jacobs: And that's where they found the mummy?

Simon Black: Yes. But this doorway had a hole in it and Carter was worried that tomb-robbers had got there first.

Fiona Jacobs: Did Carter get through this sealed doorway immediately?

Simon Black: No. There were so many precious objects in the first chamber that it took seven weeks to clear it. Carter likened it to 'a gigantic game of spillikins'. They had to be so careful not to damage the objects as they removed them.

Fiona Jacobs: So, after seven weeks, Carter was ready to break through into the burial chamber. What did he find?

Simon Black: The first thing he saw, about a yard in front of the hole he had made in the door, was a wall of gold. This turned out to be a huge shrine with three more inside it, you know, like Russian dolls. Carter said that it took 84 days of real manual labour to demolish the wall between the two chambers and dismantle the shrines.

Fiona Jacobs: So when did Carter actually see the now-famous death mask of King Tutankhamen?

Simon Black: In February, 1924. The sarcophagus was huge, 9ft in length. Carter rigged up a hoist to remove the lid that weighed over a ton and a quarter. When the lid was removed – well, let me tell you in Carter's own words: 'The light shone on the sarcophagus. The lid being suspended in mid air, we rolled back the covering shrouds, one by one, and as the last was removed, a gasp of wonderment escaped our lips, so gorgeous was the sight that met our eyes: a golden effigy of the young boy-king, of most magnificent workmanship filled the whole of the sarcophagus'. Carter was the first person to look on the face of the Pharaoh for over 3000 years.

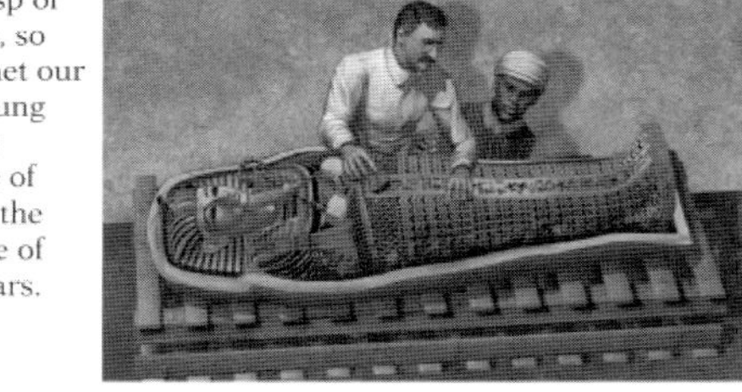

Fiona Jacobs: A fascinating story, Professor Black. Thank you.

Understanding the interview

- Who is: **a** the interviewer? **b** the interviewee?
- What is the radio programme called?
- Why was Carter sure there was a second chamber?
- Why was he worried that 'the tomb-robbers had got there first'?
- Why did they need a hoist to remove the lid?
- Find an example of:
  a a quote of what Howard Carter actually said
  b reported speech of Howard Carter's words.

Looking at words

Explain the meanings of these words and phrases as they are used in the interview:
a astounding **b** biography **c** mummy **d** precious **e** manual labour
f sarcophagus **g** hoist **h** shrouds **i** effigy

Exploring further

- What do you think Carter meant when he said that removing the objects was like 'a gigantic game of spillikins'?
- Explain why the shrines are described as being 'like Russian dolls'.
- Based on the evidence of Carter's own words at the end of the interview, how do you think everyone felt when the shrouds were removed?
- How do you think you would have felt, looking at the face of Tutankhamen and knowing that you were the first to see it for over 3000 years?
- Can you think of other 'treasures' that the radio station could make programmes about?

Extra

Imagine you could meet Howard Carter. What questions would you like to ask him?

TEACH *continued …*

- There are eight paragraphs in the article. Say briefly what each is about.
  1: Introduction of Howard Carter and his discovery; 2: The discovery; 3: Background to the discovery; 4: Getting into the tomb; 5: Details of the first treasure seen; 6: More treasure; 7: Details of the life-size statues; 8: Details of the chariots.

Plenary

- Using answers to last question, discuss the chronological structure of the article.

TALK

Before reading

- Discuss interviews with the pupils.
- What interviews have they heard / seen / read?
- Why are people interviewed?

Reading

- Explain to pupils they are going to read the transcript of a radio programme where an expert on Ancient Egypt is being interviewed. A transcript is a written copy of what was actually said.
- The extract can be read to the class by the teacher, by individuals in the class or as a group.

Discussion group

In groups, pupils discuss the questions and make notes on their responses. Ensure children understand that they do not always have to agree.

Understanding the interview

- Who is:
  a the interviewer? *Fiona Jacobs*
  b the interviewee? *Professor Simon Black*
- What is the radio programme called?
  Treasures of the Past
- Why was Carter sure there was a second chamber?
  'There was no coffin or trace of a mummy'
- Why was he worried that 'the tomb-robbers had got there first'?
  'This doorway had a hole in it'
- Why did they need a hoist to remove the lid?
  It 'weighed over a ton and a quarter'.
- Find an example of:
  a a quote of what Howard Carter actually said:
  'there was no coffin or trace of a mummy' / 'a gigantic game of spillikins' / 'The light shone on the sarcophagus … filled the whole of the sarcophagus'
  b reported speech of Howard Carter's words:
  'Carter said that it took 84 days of real manual labour to demolish the wall between the two chambers and dismantle the shrines.'

Looking at words

Explain the meaning of these words and phrases as they are used in the interview.

a ***astounding:*** *amazing / surprising;* **b** ***autobiography:*** *a personal account of one's own life;* **c** ***mummy:*** *body of a human being or animal embalmed for burial;* **d** ***precious:*** *very valuable;* **e** ***manual labour:*** *physical work with your hands;* **f** ***sarcophagus:*** *stone box for a dead body;* **g** ***hoist:*** *equipment with ropes used for lifting heavy objects;* **h** ***shrouds:*** *cloths wrapped around a dead body;* **i** ***effigy:*** *a model of someone.*

Exploring further

- What do you think Carter meant when he said that removing the objects was like 'a gigantic game of spillikins'?
  Answers that suggest that the objects were in a jumbled heap, and removing one clumsily could result in others moving or falling.
- Explain why the shrines are described as being 'like Russian dolls'.
  Answers that suggest the shrines were inside each other.
- Based on the evidence of Carter's own words at the end of the interview, how do you think everyone felt when the shrouds were removed?
  Answers that are based on evidence: 'a gasp of wonderment escaped our lips'.
- How do you think you would have felt, looking at the face of Tutankhamen and knowing that you were the first to see it for over 3000 years?
  Individual answers.
- Can you think of other 'treasures' that the radio station could make programmes about?
  Ensure all members of the group contribute ideas. One pupil should make a list.

Extra

- Imagine you could meet Howard Carter. What questions would you like to ask him?
  Ensure all members of the group contribute ideas. One pupil can take notes and the best five questions can be written in full.

About Egypt | Photos | Bookshop | Site Map

The Valley of the Kings lies on the west bank of the River Nile. To date, approximately 80 tombs have been excavated there, the most famous of which is the tomb of Tutankhamen. The Pharaohs of Egypt abandoned the practice of building pyramids as they were plundered by tomb robbers. Instead, secret tombs were dug out of the rock in the valley and the pharaohs were buried with swords, games, writing tools, oil lamps, beds, chairs – in fact everything they would need in the after-life. The tombs were then sealed and anyone who knew where they were, sworn to secrecy.

Tutankhamen was only 10 years old when he became Egypt's king. His death, in his teens, is still something of a mystery. Examination of his skull shows damage that has led some people to believe he was murdered by a blow to the head. The skeleton shows evidence of a broken leg, prompting some to say that blood poisoning from the wound was the cause of death.

However he died, his death was clearly sudden and unexpected. His tomb was too small ever to have been intended for a king when compared to that of other Pharaohs, such as Rameses II.

See also:
- The Life of Howard Carter
- Tutankhamen's Death Mask

VISIT EGYPT
www.pharaohlandhotels.co.uk

Understanding the web page

1 Where is the Valley of the Kings?
2 How many tombs have been excavated? Give two examples of things found in them.
3 How old was Tutankhamen when he became King?
4 How do people think he died?
5 The article has three paragraphs. Briefly say what each is about.

Understanding the words

6 Explain the meaning of these words and phrases as they are used in the web page:
a to date **b** excavated **c** plundered
d after-life **e** sworn to secrecy **f** prompting

Exploring the web page

7 What evidence is there that Tutankhamen's death was 'unexpected'?
8 Look at the sections at the top of the page. What would you expect to find if you clicked on:
a Photos **b** Bookshop **c** Site Map
9 Why are some of the words on the web page underlined?
10 Why do you think the page has advertisements for hotels and tours in Egypt?

Extra

- Choose one of the underlined words on the web page.
- Research it using the web or a library. Make notes.
- Prepare a report to read to the class.

TALK *continued ...*

Plenary

- Ask each group to read out their questions, and explain why they chose them.
- Ask pupils what they notice about the way the transcript is set out, and the use of direct and reported speech.

Round-up

- Discuss features of recounted text, e.g. chronological sequence / supporting illustration / degree of formality adopted.
- Pupils should be given the opportunity to read their reports to the class.

WRITE

Before reading

- Discuss what pupils use the internet for.
- Do they find it easy to use / complicated to use / useful, etc?

Reading

- Explain to pupils they are going to look at a web page about The Valley of the Kings.
- The web page can be read to the class by the teacher, by individuals in the class or individually.

Questions

Pupils answer the questions individually, drawing on their work in the previous class work (Teach) and group work (Talk).

Answer guidance

ICT

Understanding the web page

1 'on the west bank of the Nile'

2 'approximately 80 tombs'. Any two of: swords / games / writing tools / oil lamps / beds / chairs.

3 10 years old.

4 Either by a blow to the head or blood poisoning.

5 para 1: Introduction to the Valley of the Kings, Tutankhamen, pyramids and secret tombs, what was buried with the King; para 2: Details of Tutankhamen and probable causes of death; para 3: Tutankhamen's tomb.

Understanding the words

6 **a to date**: so far; **b excavated**: dug up; **c plundered**: robbed; **d after-life**: a life beyond death; **e sworn to secrecy**: made to say they would tell no one; **f prompting**: suggesting.

Exploring the web page

7 Answers that are based on the evidence: 'His tomb was too small ever to have been intended for a King…'

8 **a** Photographs of The Valley of the Kings, pyramids, Tutankhamen's tomb, Rameses II, the Nile, etc.

b Books about Egypt, Tutankhamen, The Valley of the Kings, etc.

c Layout of The Valley of the Kings with tombs marked.

9 Answers that suggest that by clicking on the underlined words, you will be taken to other pages of articles and pictures related to the topic.

10 Answers that suggest people interested in reading this page might also be interested in going to Egypt and seeing these things. Also, some pupils may know that money from advertising helps pay for putting this information on the web.

Extra

Individual answers. Try to ensure that pupils do not all choose the same area to research. If preferred, pupils can work together in pairs or groups.

Jim
Who Ran Away From His Nurse, And Was Eaten By A Lion

There was a boy whose name was Jim;
His friends were very good to him.
They gave him tea, and cakes, and jam,
And slices of delicious ham,
And chocolate with pink inside,
And little tricycles to ride,
And read him stories **through and through**,
And even took him to the Zoo –
But there it was the dreadful **fate**
Befell him, which I now **relate**.

You know – at least you ought to know,
For I have often told you so –
That children never are allowed
To leave their nurses in a crowd;
Now this was Jim's especial **foible**,
He ran away when he was able,
And on this **inauspicious** day
He slipped his hand and ran away!
He hadn't gone a yard when – Bang!
With open jaws, a lion sprang,
And hungrily began to eat
The boy: beginning at his feet.

Now, just imagine how it feels
When first your toes and then your heels,
And then by gradual degrees,
Your shins and ankles, calves and knees,
Are slowly eaten, bit by bit.
No wonder Jim **detested** it!
No wonder that he shouted 'Hi!'
The honest keeper heard his cry,
Though very fat he almost ran
To help the little gentleman.
'Ponto!' he ordered as he came
(For Ponto was the lion's name),
'Ponto!' he cried, with angry frown.

'Let go, Sir! Down, Sir! Put it down!'
The lion made a sudden stop,
He let the dainty **morsel** drop,
And **slunk reluctant** to his cage,
Snarling with disappointed rage,
But when he bent him over Jim,
The honest keeper's eyes were dim.
The lion having reached his head,
The miserable boy was dead!

When Nurse informed his parents, they
Were more concerned than I can say: –
His Mother, as she dried her eyes,
Said, 'Well – it gives me no surprise,
He would not do as he was told!'
His Father, who was self-controlled,
Bade all the children round **attend**
To James's miserable end,
And always keep a-hold of Nurse
For fear of finding something worse.

'Jim Who Ran Away From His Nurse,
And Was Eaten By A Lion' from *Cautionary Tales for Children*,
Hilaire Belloc (this edition from *The Nation's Favourite Children's Poems*)

- Who is the main character in the poem?
- How do you know that his friends were 'very good to him'?
- What other characters are introduced as the story is told?
- Where was the main character when something 'dreadful' happened?
- Explain the meaning of the words and phrases in **bold** as they are used in the poem.
- Find phrases where the poet talks directly to the reader.
- Why do you think he does this?
- What impression do you get of:
  - the Nurse
  - the Keeper
  - Jim's mother and father?
- Do you think the poem is 'serious' or 'funny'? Explain your reasons.

Extracts

Jim – Who Ran Away From His Nurse, And Was Eaten By A Lion Hilaire Belloc
The Apple-Raid Vernon Scannell
Early Last Sunday Morning Ian Souter

Planning

Narrative poems

Objectives

Renewed Primary Literacy Framework Year 5
3 *Group discussion and interaction*
- Understand different ways to take the lead and support others in groups.

4 *Drama*
- Reflect on how working in role helps to explore complex issues.

5 *Engaging with and responding to texts*
- Compare how a common theme is presented in poetry.

7 *Understanding and interpreting texts*
- Use evidence from across a text to explain events.
- Explore how writers use language for comic and dramatic effect.

Assessment focuses
AF5 Explain and comment on writer's use of language, including grammatical and literary features
L3–L5 Identify features of writer's use of language and increasingly comment on writer's choices.
AF7 Relate texts to social, cultural and historical traditions
L3/L4/L5 Make connections between texts, increasingly identifying common and different features, recognise and make comments on context.

Scottish Curriculum for Excellence: Literacy
Listening and Talking
Tools for listening and talking (third/fourth levels)
Can respond in ways appropriate to their role and use contributions to reflect on, clarify or adapt thinking; can explore and expand on contributions.
Reading
Understanding, analysing and evaluating (third/fourth levels)
Can identify and discuss similarities and differences and compare and contrast different types of text.

TEACH

In this unit pupils will investigate a 'classic' narrative poem by Hilaire Belloc, and two other poems which don't 'tell a story' in the traditional sense, but relate an incident / experience that takes place over a small amount of time. All three poems contain features of a narrative, such as characters, plot and setting.

Before reading

- What do pupils understand by the term 'cautionary tale'?
- What do they understand by the term 'narrative'?
- What cautionary tales do they know? (Possibly Aesop's fables.)

Reading

- Explain that pupils are going to read a 'cautionary tale' told in the form of a 'narrative' poem. It is called *'Jim – Who Ran Away From His Nurse, And Was Eaten By A Lion'*. Based on the title, what lesson do they think it is teaching?
- The poem can be read to the class by the teacher, by individuals in the class or individually.

After reading

Use the panel prompts in the Pupil Book as the basis of a class discussion.

- Who is the main character in the poem? *Jim.*
- How do you know that his friends were 'very good to him'?
  Answers that are based on evidence: 'gave him tea and cakes and jam' / 'slices of delicious ham' / 'chocolate with pink inside' / 'little tricycles to ride'.
- What other characters are introduced as the story is told?
  The Nurse, Ponto the lion, Jim's mother and father.
- Where was the main character when something 'dreadful' happened?
  At the Zoo.
- Explain the meaning of the words and phrases in bold as they are used in the poem:
  through and through: *over and over again;* ***fate:*** *something that is going to happen;* ***befell:*** *happened (to him);* ***relate:*** *tell;* ***foible:*** *weakness / bad habit;* ***inauspicious:*** *unlucky;* ***detested:*** *hated;* ***morsel:*** *very small piece;* ***slunk reluctant:*** *moved away guiltily but didn't want to go;* ***bade:*** *ordered;* ***attend:*** *listen.*
- Find phrases where the poet talks directly to the reader.
  'You know – at least you ought to know, For I have often told you so' / 'Now, just imagine how it feels When first your toes and then your heels…'
- Why do you think he does this?
  Answers that suggest that the poem is 'teaching' something, and that the poet wants to create the impression that he is telling this face to face.
- What impression do you get of the Nurse, the Keeper, Jim's mother and father?
  Nurse: careless / not very concerned about Jim;
  Keeper: kind / tries to help / upset when he can't save Jim;
  mother and father: mother upset but not as much as you would expect! Jim's father doesn't seem upset at all!

The Apple-Raid

Darkness came early, though not yet cold;
Stars were strung on the telegraph wires;
Street lamps spilled pools of liquid gold;
The breeze was spiced with garden fires.

That smell of burnt leaves, the early dark,
Can still excite me but not as it did
So long ago when we met in the park –
Myself, John Peters and David Kidd.

We moved out of town to the district where
The lucky and wealthy had their homes
With garages, gardens, and apples to spare
Ripely clustered in the trees' green domes.

We chose this place we meant to plunder
And climbed the wall and dropped down to
The secret dark. Apples crunched under
Our feet as we moved through the grass and dew.

The clusters on the lower boughs of the tree
Were easy to reach. We stored the fruit
In pockets and jerseys until all three
Boys were heavy with their tasty loot.

Safe on the other side of the wall
We moved back to town and munched as we went.
I wonder if David remembers at all
That little adventure, the apples' fresh scent.

Strange to think that he's fifty years old,
That tough little boy with scabs on his knees;
Stranger to think that John Peters lies cold
In an orchard in France beneath apple trees.

'The Apple-Raid', Vernon Scannell

Understanding the poem

- Who 'met in the park'?
- What did they do?
- From what part of the tree did they steal the fruit?
- How did they carry it?
- How do you know that what the poet is describing happened a long time ago?

Looking at words

Explain the meaning of these words and phrases as they are used in the poem:

a spiced **b** district **c** clustered **d** plunder **e** loot **f** lies cold

Exploring further

- In which season of the year do you think the apple-raid took place? Give your reasons.
- Why do you think the boys went 'out of town' to steal apples?
- Look at these descriptions: 'liquid gold', 'green domes', 'the secret dark'.
  a Say what each is describing.
  b Do you think it is a good description? Why? Why not?
- Why do you think John Peters 'lies cold' in France?
- How do you think the poet feels when he remembers 'that little adventure'?

Extra

Act out the poem from when the boys meet in the park to when they return to town. Think about what the boys would say and do during 'that little adventure'.

TEACH *continued …*

- Do you think the poem is 'serious' or 'funny'? Explain your reasons.
  Answers that suggest the poem is 'funny', although teaching a valuable lesson.

Plenary

- Did the children enjoy the poem? Why? Why not?
- Were they right about what the poem is teaching? (See 'Reading' on page 65.)

TALK

Before reading

- Explain to pupils that a narrative poem, as well as having a plot, characters and dialogue, can also capture a short event or moment in time that lives in the memory.
- Can they think of something they have done that would make a good narrative poem?

Reading

- Explain to pupils that they are going to read a narrative poem called 'The Apple-Raid'. In it, the poet tells the story of a vivid memory from childhood.
- The poem can be read to the class by the teacher, by individuals in the class or as a group.

Discussion group

In groups, pupils discuss the questions and make notes on their responses. Ensure pupils understand that they do not always have to agree.

Understanding the poem

- Who 'met in the park'?
  'Myself [the poet], John Peters and David Kidd'.
- What did they do?
  They left the town and went to a 'smarter' district, chose a garden and stole apples.
- From what part of the tree did they steal the fruit?
  'the lower boughs of the tree'
- How did they carry it?
  'In pockets and jerseys'
- How do you know that what the poet is describing happened a long time ago?
  'Strange to think he's [David] fifty years old' / 'John Peters lies cold'

Looking at words

Explain the meaning of these words and phrases as they are used in the poem.

a *spiced:* *made to smell spicy / tangy;* **b *district:*** *area;* **c *clustered:*** *lots grouped together;* **d *plunder:*** *rob;* **e *loot:*** *things that have been stolen;* **f *lies cold:*** *is dead.*

Exploring further

- In which season of the year do you think the apple-raid took place? Give your reasons.
  Answers that suggest autumn – 'Darkness came early, though not yet cold' / 'burnt leaves' / apples on trees.
- Why do you think the boys went 'out of town' to steal apples?
  Answers that suggest that houses in the town did not have gardens so there were no apple trees.
- Look at these descriptions.
  a Say what each is describing.
  'liquid gold': light from street lamps;
  'green domes': the leafy branches of the apple trees;
  'the secret dark': the garden.
  b Do you think it is a good description? Why? Why not?
  Individual answers.
- Why do you think John Peters 'lies cold' in France?
  Pupils are likely to say that he went to France to live. Ask them to explore the possibility of other reasons he is buried in France, e.g. died in the war.
- How do you think the poet feels when he remembers 'that little adventure'? ICT
  Answers that suggest he feels nostalgic / he enjoys reliving the adventure / sadness to think so many years have passed.

Extra

ICT

- Act out the poem from when the boys met in the park to when they returned to town. Think about what the boys would say and do during 'that little adventure'.
  Ensure all members of the group contribute ideas and take part in the performance. Emphasise that they should think carefully about the different feelings the boys would experience: meeting up; on the way out of town; stealing the apples; getting away without being caught.

Plenary

- Let each group act out the poem for the class.

Early Last Sunday Morning

Early last Sunday morning
Dad announced we needed a glass of fresh air
and a mouthful of greenness.
So we slipped off to the nearby park
where we crept in as soundless as snails.
Around us the day breathed air
that was as sharp as vinegar
reminding us that winter was well on its way.

Inside we watched the trees stretch and wake
while the grass stood up and shivered.
Soon I was pointing towards a spider
that was strung on a necklace web
while far behind it
the sun rolled out like a golden ball.

Suddenly Dad smiled
as a squirrel scampered from a bush
then turned to grey stone
until with a flick of its tail
it waved goodbye and was gone.

Later as we passed the children's playground
I looked at the lonely, red slide
and briefly remembered the summer days
when I flew its slippery, red tongue.
But a tug of wind pushed me past
Until I just let the warmth in Dad's hand
finally lead me on towards home.

'Early Last Sunday Morning', Ian Souter

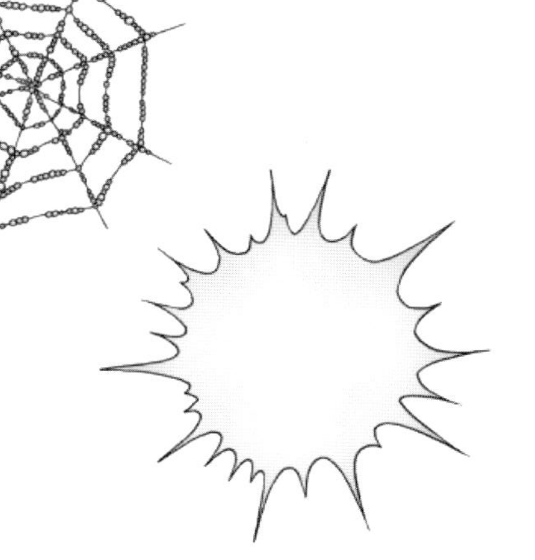

Understanding the poem

1 What is the setting for the poem?
2 Who are the characters in the poem?
3 In what season does the poem take place?
4 What living things does the poet see?
5 What has the poet played on in the children's playground?

Understanding the words

6 Explain the meaning of these words and phrases as they are used in the poem:
a announced **b** well on its way **c** scampered
d flick **e** briefly **f** tug

Exploring the poem

7 Explain in your own words why Dad thought it was a good idea to go to the park.
8 Look at these similes: 'soundless as snails', 'sharp as vinegar'.
a What is each simile describing?
b Do you think they are good descriptions? Why? Why not?
9 What does the poet mean when he:
a says that the squirrel 'turned to grey stone';
b describes the slide as 'lonely'?
10 How do you think the poet felt about the trip to the park with his Dad? Explain your reasons.

Extra

Imagine that you are the poet. Write a short description of what you did and how you felt 'early last Sunday morning'.

WRITE

 Before reading

- Discuss what pupils do on a Sunday.

Reading

- Explain to pupils they are going to read a poem called 'Early Last Sunday Morning', in which the poet narrates a trip to the park with his Dad. Read the poem.
- The poem can be read to the class by the teacher, by individuals in the class or individually.

 Questions

Pupils answer the questions individually, drawing on their work in the previous class work (Teach) and group work (Talk).

Round-up

- Pupils compare the three narrative poems. In what way are they similar and different? Which one do pupils like the best? Why?

Answer guidance

Understanding the poem

1 The park.
2 The poet (narrator) and his Dad.
3 Late autumn – 'winter was well on its way'.
4 Squirrel, spider.
5 The slide.

Understanding the words

6 **a announced**: said quite determinedly; **b well on its way**: almost here; **c scampered**: moved quickly with small steps; **d flick**: a quick, sudden movement; **e briefly**: for a moment; **f tug**: a strong, short pull

ICT

Exploring the poem

7 Answers that suggest they had been indoors for a long time and needed to get some fresh air.
8 **a** How they crept into the park; the coldness of the air.
b Individual answers.
9 **a** Answers that suggest the squirrel stood so still it looked as if it had turned to stone.
b Answers that suggest no one is playing in the park or on the slide.
10 Individual answers – suggestions could be that the narrator is happy to be with his Dad and to see such a range of things; or a little sad at the emptiness of the once busy playground, and the passing of summer.

Extra

Individual answers.

A new school

Next morning Martine woke feeling as if she was going to the dentist. For a long time she lay there with her eyes screwed tightly shut, because that way she could pretend that none of it had happened. Her home had not burned down, and her mum and dad were not gone forever, and she had not been sent to the wilds of Africa to live with a total stranger. Finally, when she could avoid it no longer, she opened her eyes. A **vast** sky of the most **incredible** blue filled her vision. The clock on the bedside table said 6.05 a.m. Right on cue, an orange-breasted bird fluttered onto a thatch beam outside her window and began singing a song of pure happiness. *Tirrootiree, tirrootiree.*

Propping herself up on one elbow, Martine gazed out over the game reserve. The waterhole was draped with early morning mist and streaked with gold from the sun. A dozen or so elephants were splashing around in it, **wallowing** in the mud and spraying each other with their trunks. Zebras were grazing nearby. She shook her head in wonder. The scene didn't take away the **anguish** in her heart, but it definitely helped.

Even so, she walked downstairs on leaden feet. Her grandmother was sitting at the kitchen table, her hands wrapped around a coffee mug. When Martine entered, she stood up quickly and said: 'Good morning, Martine, I hope you slept well.' Her voice shook slightly, as though she was nervous. Before Martine could speak, she went on hurriedly: 'There is a boiled egg in the pan and some bread in the toaster and anything else you might need on the kitchen table. On the counter over there, you'll find a lunchbox containing sunscreen, yellow cling peaches from the garden and some cheese and chutney sandwiches. I have to go out now to feed the young elephant, but I'll be back at 7.30 to take you to school.'

Martine was still stammering a thank you when the stable door banged behind her grandmother and a gust of cool air blew in. It wasn't an apology, but Martine already knew that was all she was going to get.

The dentist feeling returned on the fifteen-minute drive to school, most of which Martine spent **squirming** in her new uniform, hating the skirt and not knowing what to say to her grandmother. And it didn't **diminish** when Gwyn Thomas drove her through the gates of Caracal Junior and she saw the **hordes** of healthy, confident children who were to be her new schoolmates. They were every shade of honey, cappuccino and chocolate. None were the colour of Martine – that is to say, a sort of unhealthy grey-white. After her grandmother had left her at the door of the headmistress's office with a gruff but kindly 'Have a good day. Tendai or I will collect you at four,' she stood pressed against the wall, trying to be as **inconspicuous** as possible.

'Be with you in a mo,' called a voice when she knocked. Martine could hear someone speaking on the phone. While she waited, she took in her surroundings. Her old school, Bodley Brook, had resembled a concrete prison, with a tarmac playground and peeling beige corridors, reeking of disinfectant. The toilets had been covered in graffiti. This school didn't even look like a school. It was more like a lovely campsite. Log buildings made from glowing chestnut timber were scattered about grounds laid with emerald lawns and huge trees. Behind a wooden fence, a swimming pool sparkled.

'You can close your mouth now. We still have the same boring old lessons you had back home. You know, long division, dead kings, punctuation!'

The expression on Martine's face must have said it all, because the Cleopatra-haired vision standing in the doorway wearing wooden parrot earrings and a long purple dress laughed merrily and, pulling her into the room, added: 'Only joking. Our lessons are, of course, extremely interesting. I'm Elaine Rathmore, the headmistress, and you must be Martine. Welcome to Caracal Junior.'

From *The White Giraffe*,
Lauren St John

- Who are the characters in this part of the story?
- What are the three settings in the extract?
- Why had Martine 'been sent to Africa to live with a total stranger'?
- What is the name of Martine's new school?
- Explain the meaning of the words in **bold** as they are used in the extract.
- What do you think the author means when she writes that Martine felt 'as if she was going to the dentist', and walked downstairs 'on leaden feet'?
- Why do you think Martine's lunchbox contains sunscreen?
- Martine arrived at the game reserve the day before. Find evidence in the extract that shows her first meeting with her grandmother had not gone well.
- What is your impression of:
  a Martine's grandmother?
  b Elaine Rathmore?
- How do you think Martine was feeling:
  – when she woke up;
  – during the drive to school;
  – at school?

Extracts

The White Giraffe Lauren St John
Jeffie Lemmington and me Merle Hodge
Walkabout James Vance Marshall

Planning

Exploring stories from around the world

Objectives

Renewed Primary Literacy Framework Year 5

3 *Group discussion and interaction*
- Understand different ways to take the lead and support others in groups.

4 *Drama*
- Reflect on how working in role helps to explore complex issues.

7 *Understanding and interpreting texts*
- Use evidence from text to explain events or ideas.
- Infer writer's (character's) perspective from what is written and what is implied.

Assessment focuses

AF3 Deduce, infer or interpret information, events or ideas from texts
L3 Begin to interpret character and motives using text
L4 Show understanding of character and motives through explanation and prediction
L5 Use full range of evidence to comment on characters and motives.

AF7 Relate texts to social, cultural and historical traditions
L3–L5 Increasingly make connections between texts, identifying common features and differences; recognise and make simple comments on social and cultural context.

Scottish Curriculum for Excellence: Literacy
Listening and Talking
Tools for listening and talking (third level)
Make relevant contributions when engaging with others, encourage others to contribute and acknowledge that they have the right to hold a different opinion.
Reading
Finding and using information (third and fourth levels)
Can make notes and organise them to explore issues and create new texts, using own words as appropriate.

TEACH

This unit takes a different angle on the genre of 'other cultures'. Instead of providing straightforward stories from other cultures, pupils will investigate characters who are moved into another culture by force of circumstances.

Before reading

- What do pupils understand by the term 'game reserve'?
- Where would they expect to find one?
- What do they know about Africa?

Reading

- Explain to pupils they are going to read an extract from a story called *The White Giraffe*. It is set on a game reserve in Africa. The main character, Martine, used to live in England with her parents. They were killed in a fire and Martine has been sent to live with her grandmother, who runs a game reserve in Africa. The extract begins on Martine's first morning in her new home.
- The extract can be read to the class by the teacher, by individuals in the class or individually.

After reading

ICT

Use the panel prompts in the Pupil Book as the basis of a class discussion.

- Who are the characters in this part of the story?
  Martine; her Grandmother; Elaine Rathmore.
- What are the three settings in the extract?
  The game reserve; the car journey; the school.
- Why had Martine 'been sent to Africa to live with a total stranger'?
  Her home had 'burned down' and 'her mum and dad were gone forever'.
- What is the name of Martine's new school?
  Caracal Junior.
- Explain the meaning of the words in bold as they are used in the extract:
  vast: *extremely large;* ***incredible:*** *unbelievable;* ***wallowing:*** *rolling about;* ***anguish:*** *grief / emotional pain;* ***squirming:*** *twisting and turning in discomfort;* ***diminish:*** *grow less;* ***hordes:*** *a large number;* ***inconspicuous:*** *unnoticeable.*
- What do you think the author means when she writes that Martine felt 'as if she was going to the dentist', and walked downstairs with 'leaden feet'?
  Answers that suggest Martine had a sense of dread, was reluctant to go downstairs and therefore walked very slowly.
- Why do you think Martine's lunchbox contains sunscreen?
  Answers that suggest that the sun in Africa is very hot and she would need protection.
- Martine arrived at the game reserve the day before. Find evidence in the extract that shows her first meeting with her grandmother had not gone well.
  Martine wasn't looking forward to going downstairs.
  She obviously felt her grandmother had something to apologise for. 'It wasn't an apology, but Martine ...'.
  Martine is also left to have breakfast alone, and there is no conversation on the way to school.

Snowfall

The narrator was born in the West Indies. His parents moved to England and left him with his grandmother and his uncle. Later on, he joined his parents, who he could not remember, and his brother, who he had never seen.

I was seven and I had thought that snow was like cotton wool, so I had always wondered how the children in books made snowmen stand up without the breeze blowing them away.

When my mother woke me up one morning, she said, 'There's snow darling, come and see!'

We stood at the window looking down. The tops of the parked cars were covered with thick white hair, as though they had grown old in the night. The pavement was covered with it, too, and the roof – the long row of joined-together roofs – of the opposite side of the street, everything. It was very mysterious. A giant had come and quietly laid his fluffy white towel down over the whole street and vanished again.

My mother was holding me. 'Pretty, eh?' she said. I did not answer. Instead I squirmed with shyness. I was shy of my mother. I did not know my mother, I did not know my father, and – I did not trust the little boy they had with them who did not talk like me and didn't seem to feel cold, who they said was my little brother.

I had looked forward to seeing my little brother. When I was going to take the plane, Granny had given me a paper bag full of sweets to bring for him. And he had sniffed and nibbled at them, screwing up his face, and handed them back to my mother.

In the night when I was falling asleep, or when I woke up in the middle of the night, then this place seemed to be a dream that I was having. It was always close and dark here, as in a dream, and there was no midday; the whole day was the same colour. And you could never just scamper out through the front door if you felt like it, you first had to pile on all those clothes that made you feel heavier than when you had got soaked in the rain.

But when I was up and about, then it was Granny and Uncle Nello who seemed to be tucked away in a dream somewhere, or in some bright yellow storybook.

Granny was both sad and happy when they'd written and said that I could go to them now. Happy for me because at last I was going Up There. They were rather put out when I announced that I wasn't going anywhere. I hadn't the slightest interest in my mother and father – only when I got parcels from them with sweets and toys; but when I had gobbled up the sweets and broken the toys or exchanged them for things my friends had, then I forgot about my mother and father until the next parcel came.

But I didn't mind going Up There to have a look at this little brother who seemed to have crept into the world behind my back, for Granny and Uncle Nello said that I had never seen him. (They also said that I *had* seen my mother and father and that they had seen me, but I knew they were only fooling me.)

And now I had come to this uncomfortable place, and I had seen my little brother, and now I was ready to go back to Granny and Uncle Nello.

From *Jeffie Lemmington and Me*, Merle Hodge

Understanding the extract

- How old was the narrator when he first saw snow?
- How does he feel: **a** when he is with his mother and father? **b** about his brother?
- When he lived with Granny, when was the only time he was interested in his parents?
- What was the only reason he agreed to go 'Up There'?

Looking at words

Explain the meaning of these words and phrases as they are used in the extract:

a mysterious　**b** vanished　**c** scamper
d put out　**e** slightest　**f** behind my back

Exploring further

- The narrator describes the snow as 'cotton wool', 'thick white hair' and a 'fluffy white towel'. Which description do you think is the best? Why?
- Find evidence in the extract that suggests the narrator and his brother are not going to get along.
- Explain in your own words how the narrator feels at night.
- Why do you think the narrator thinks of Granny and Uncle Nello as being in a 'bright yellow storybook'?
- Who do you think the narrator feels is his real family? Why does he think this?

Extra

Imagine you could meet the narrator of this story.
What questions would you like to ask him?

TEACH *continued ...*

- What is your impression of:

  a Martine's grandmother?

  Answers that are based on evidence: 'Her voice shook slightly as if she was nervous'. Also, she is practical and thoughtful (she has prepared the lunch box).

  b Elaine Rathmore?

  Answers that are based on evidence that she has a sense of humour ('long division, dead kings, punctuation') and is very friendly and informal, e.g. 'Be with you in a mo'.

- How do you think Martine was feeling when she woke up; during the drive to school; at school?

  Answers based on evidence from the text:

  When she woke up: 'feeling as if she was going to the dentist'; 'anguish in her heart'.

  During the drive to school: 'The dentist feeling returned ...'

  At school: 'And it didn't diminish ...'; 'trying to be as inconspicuous as possible.'

Plenary

- How would pupils feel in Martine's situation?
- Discuss what differences there would be if the extract was told from the grandmother's point of view.

TALK

Before reading

- Ask pupils to imagine that they had not seen their parents for such a long time that they could not remember them.
- How would they feel when they met them again?
- What would they say and do?

Reading

- Explain to pupils that they are going to read the beginning of a story called *Jeffie Lemmington and me*. (Jeffie Lemmington does not appear in this part of the story.) The narrator remembers when he was seven years old and saw snow for the first time.
- The extract can be read to the class by the teacher, by individuals in the class or as a group.

Discussion group

In groups, pupils discuss the questions and make notes on their responses. Ensure pupils understand that they do not always have to agree.

Understanding the extract

- How old was the narrator when he first saw snow? *Seven years old.*
- How does he feel:

  a when he is with his mother and father? *Shy*

  b about his brother?

  - Before he arrived:

    'I had looked forward to seeing my little brother'
  - Now:

    'I did not trust the little boy'
- When he lived with Granny, when was the only time he was interested in his parents?

  When 'I got parcels from them with sweets and toys'.
- What was the only reason he agreed to go 'Up There'?

  'To have a look at this little brother'

Looking at words

Explain the meaning of these words and phrases as they are used in the extract:

a ***mysterious:*** *strange;* **b** ***vanished:*** *disappeared;* **c** ***scamper:*** *run out;* **d** ***put out:*** *disappointed and slightly annoyed;* **e** ***slightest:*** *least;* **f** ***behind my back:*** *without me knowing (in a sneaky way).*

Exploring further

- The narrator describes the snow as 'cotton wool', 'thick white hair' and a 'fluffy white towel'. Which description do you think is the best? Why?

  Individual answers.

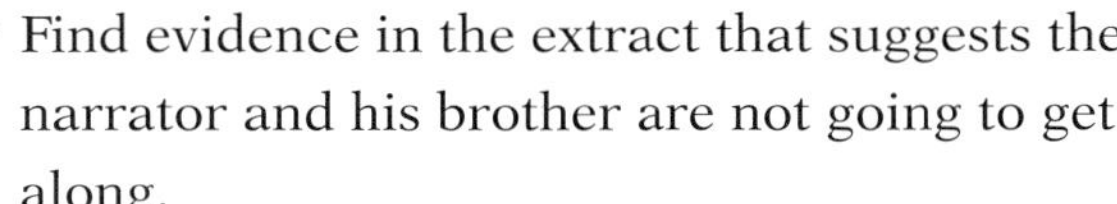

ICT

- Find evidence in the extract that suggests the narrator and his brother are not going to get along.

  'I did not trust the little boy they had with them who did not talk like me…' / When the narrator gives him sweets 'he had sniffed and nibbled them, screwing up his face, and handed them back to my mother'.
- Explain in your own words how the narrator feels at night.

  Answers that suggest he was homesick – 'this place seemed to be a dream' / 'the whole day was the same colour'.
- Why do you think the narrator thinks of Granny and Uncle Nello as being in a 'bright yellow storybook'?

  Answers that suggest the narrator remembers the world he has come from as colourful and full of sunshine.

Walkabout

Mary and Peter are on their way to their Uncle Keith in Adelaide. They are the only passengers on a small cargo plane that crashes in the Australian desert. They are the only survivors.

It was silent and dark, and the children were afraid. They huddled together, their backs to an outcrop of rock. Far below them, in the bed of the gully, a little stream flowed inland – soon to peter out in the vastness of the Australian desert. Above them the walls of the gully climbed smoothly to a moonless sky.

The little boy nestled more closely against his sister. He was trembling.

She felt for his hand, and held it, very tightly.

'All right, Peter,' she whispered. 'I'm here.'

She felt the tension ebb slowly out of him, the trembling die gradually away. When a boy is only eight a big sister of thirteen can be wonderfully comforting.

'Mary,' he whispered, 'I'm hungry. Let's have something to eat.'

The girl sighed. She felt in the pocket of her frock, and pulled out a paper-covered stick of barley sugar. It was their last one. She broke it, gave him half, and slipped the other half back in her pocket.

'Don't bite,' she whispered. 'Suck.'

Why they were whispering they didn't know. Perhaps because everything was so very silent: like a church. Or was it because they were afraid; afraid of being heard?

For a while the only sounds were the distant rippling of water over stone, and the sucking of lips around a diminishing stick of barley sugar. Then the boy started to fidget, moving restlessly from one foot to another. Again the girl reached for his hand.

'Aren't you comfy, Pete?'

'No.'

'What is it?'

'My leg's bleeding again. I can feel the wet.'

She bent down. The handkerchief that she had tied round his thigh was now draped like a recalcitrant garter over his ankle. She refastened it, and they huddled together, holding hands, looking into the powdery blackness of the Australian night.

They could see nothing. They could hear nothing – apart from the lilt of the rivulet – for it was still too early for the stirring of bush life. Later there'd be other sounds; the hoot of the mopoke, the mating howl of the dingo, and the leathery flip-flap-flip of the wings of flying foxes. But now, an hour after sunset, the bush was silent: frighteningly still: full, to the children, of terrors all the greater for being unknown. It was a far cry from here to their comfortable home in Charleston, South Carolina.

The hours meandered past, like slow, unhurrying snails. At last the boy's head dropped to his sister's lap. He snuggled closer. His breathing became slower, deeper. He slept.

But the girl didn't sleep…

From *Walkabout*, James Vance Marshall

Understanding the extract

1 Where has the plane crashed?

2 Which of the children is the oldest?

3 Where has Peter been hurt?

4 Give two examples of animals that would make noises during the night.

Understanding the words

5 Explain the meaning of these words and phrases as they are used in the extract:

a gully	**b** vastness	**c** tension
d ebb slowly	**e** diminishing	**f** recalcitrant
g a far cry	**h** meandered	

Exploring further

6 What impression do you get of:
a Mary? **b** Peter?

7 Why do you think Mary told Peter to 'suck' the barley sugar instead of biting it?

8 Why do you think she put the other half of the barley sugar in her pocket?

9 What do you think the author means when he says that the 'terrors' were 'all the greater for being unknown'?

10 Why do you think Mary didn't sleep?

Extra

Imagine you are Mary. Peter has fallen asleep. You have no food, it is night, and you are lost. Make notes on:

- how you are feeling
- what you are thinking about
- what you are planning to do.

TALK *continued …*

- Who do you think the narrator feels is his real family? Why does he think this?
  Answers suggesting that he feels Granny and Uncle Nello are his real family, based on evidence: 'They were rather put out when I announced that I wasn't going anywhere' / 'They also said I had seen my mother and father and that they had seen me, but I knew they were only fooling me' / 'now I was ready to go back to Granny and Uncle Nello'.

Extra

ICT

Imagine you could meet the narrator of this story. What questions would you like to ask him?

Ensure all members of the group contribute questions. One pupil should take notes.

Plenary

- Use groups' ideas for the 'Extra' activity as a basis for a class discussion.
- Discuss how the story would be different if told from the little brother's point of view.

WRITE

Before reading

- What do pupils know about Australia?
- Have any of them ever visited Australia?
- What kind of landscape would they find over most of the country?

Reading

- Explain to pupils they are going to read the beginning of a story called *Walkabout*, which is set in the Australian desert.
- The extract can be read to the class by the teacher, by individuals in the class or individually.

Questions

Pupils answer the questions individually, drawing on their work in the previous class work (Teach) and group work (Talk).

Answer guidance

ICT

Understanding the extract

1 The Australian desert.
2 Mary.
3 His thigh.
4 Two from: mopoke, dingo, flying foxes.

Understanding the words

5 **a gully**: a river valley; **b vastness**: huge size; **c tension**: a feeling of being so worried that you cannot relax; **d ebb slowly**: go away gradually; **e diminishing**: decreasing / growing smaller; **f recalcitrant**: disobedient; **g a far cry**: a long way (in distance and surroundings); **h meandered**: moved slowly.

Exploring further

6 **a** Answers suggesting that she is caring and feels responsible for her brother based on evidence: 'she felt for his hand, and held it, tightly' / 'All right Peter, I'm here' / 'Are you comfy?' / She tied the handkerchief around Peter's wound.

b Answers suggesting that he is dependent on his sister and is very afraid based on evidence: 'He was trembling' / 'the trembling died gradually away' / 'When a boy is only eight a big sister of thirteen can be wonderfully comforting'.

7 Answers that suggest she wanted Peter to make it to last as long as possible because it was their only food.
8 Answers that suggest she was going to eat it later OR that she was saving it for Peter.
9 Answers suggesting that if you don't know exactly what is frightening you, your imagination can make it much worse than it actually is.
10 Answer suggesting that she stayed awake to watch over Peter.

Extra

Look for children to express the feelings they imagine they would have in such an isolated and alien environment; what they would be thinking about and ideas for escaping their situation.

Round-up

- Use pupils' answers to the 'Extra' activity as a basis for a class discussion.
- Compare the situations in which the children find themselves in the three extracts. What are the similarities and differences?

Are you convinced?

▸ **Exploring persuasive language**

STAYHEALTHY MAGAZINE

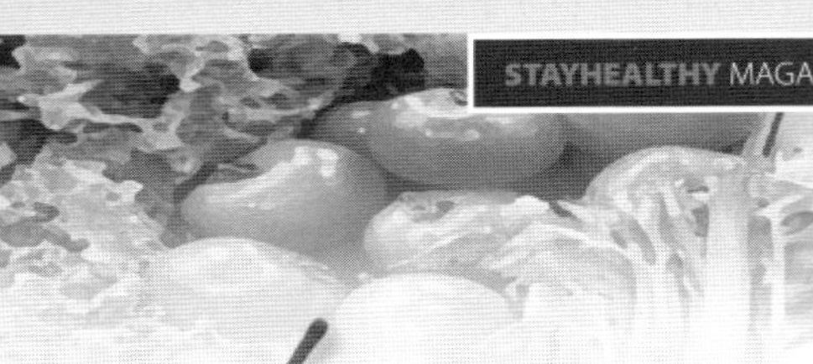

You are what you eat

Do you think the food you eat affects your health? Well, scientists have given us every reason to believe that to be true, but we still seem to be ignoring them.

Walk along any high street and count the number of fast-food **establishments** that offer over-priced and under-nourishing **fare** that we are quite happy to **contaminate** our bodies with: burgers, chips, fizzy drinks and all the other items appropriately named 'junk food'.

So what should we be eating to live long and stay healthy? Let's look at just a few of the discoveries of the past few months that it would **benefit** us all to take notice of.

Take the simple almond. It has been discovered that a few almonds every day can fight cancer and heart disease. This miracle nut contains flavanoids that not only help beat cancer, but also can fight the ageing process. Not something a plate of chips can do!

And what about the apple that helps you live longer? The bitter English apple called Evesse is no longer eaten today but it should be. Its amazing ingredient, epicatechin, boosts the heart and circulation. Scientists are very excited about this discovery and you will soon be able to buy it as a juice and a sweetener.

Lifestyle

STAYHEALTHY MAGAZINE

And lastly, the humble grape. Tests have shown that within the seeds of this little fruit is an ingredient that will kill lots of leukaemia cells quickly!

So, burgers, chips and pizza, or almonds, apples and grapes? No one but a complete idiot would continue to ignore what science is telling us. And what do you notice about the healthy food? Yes, it's all natural. Not an **E-number** in sight, and no trace of the dreaded monosodium glutamate.

Do yourself a favour – and, more importantly, do your children a favour – and change your eating habits today. Set a good example and make sure your kids eat their five portions of fruit and vegetables every day. Give them a chance at a long, healthy life and bin the junk food.

The Association of Fruit and Vegetables for a Healthy Life

Other Miracle Foods

Cooked tomatoes
Help the skin fight sunburn

Blackberries
Protect against heart disease and cancer

Spinach
Combats eye disease and anaemia

Tea
Helps reduce blood pressure

Lifestyle

Teach

- What is the writer trying to persuade you to do?
- Name three healthy and three unhealthy foods.
- Who has written the article?
- Explain the meanings of the **bold** words as they are used in the article.
- Explain in your own words what the title of the article means.
- Why do you think the writer begins with a question?
- Why do you think the writer mentions 'scientists' several times?
- Why do you think the writer uses the phrase 'no one but a complete idiot'?
- Do you think it is important to know who wrote the article or not? Explain your reasons.
- Are you persuaded by this article? Why? Why not?

Extracts

You are what you eat
Letter commenting on 'You are what you eat'
Outlaw sunbeds plea as cases of skin cancer soar

Planning

Persuasive texts

Objectives

Renewed Primary Literacy Framework Year 5

1 *Speaking*
- Present a spoken argument, sequencing points logically, defending views, and using persuasive language.

2 *Listening and responding*
- Analyse the use of persuasive language.

7 *Understanding and interpreting texts*
- Use evidence from across the text to explain events.
- Infer writers' perspectives from what is written and what is implied.

Assessment focuses

AF5 Explain and comment on writer's use of language at word and sentence level
L3 Identify a few features of writer's use of language
L4 Make simple comments on the writer's choices
L5 Show some awareness of the effect of writer's language choices.

AF6 Identify and comment on writer's purposes and viewpoints, and the overall effect of the text on the reader
L3–L5 Increasingly identify purpose and viewpoint, and be aware of and explain the effect on reader.

Scottish Curriculum for Excellence: Literacy

Listening and Talking
Understanding, analysing and evaluating (third/fourth levels)
Develop an informed view through learning about the techniques used to influence opinion; learn how to asses the value of different sources.

Reading
Understanding, analysing and evaluating (third/fourth levels)
Learn about techniques used to influence opinion, persuasion and bias, and assess the reliability of information and the credibility and value of different sources.

TEACH

This is the second of two units on persuasive texts. In this unit pupils will study three texts linked by the theme of healthy living. The first is a newspaper article that appears convincing but, on closer inspection, has little foundation; the second is a letter commenting on the article and highlighting its shortcomings; the final article has more 'weight' and is more persuasive, as expert sources and startling statistics are cited.

Before reading

Discuss 'healthy eating' with pupils.

- What do they think of as healthy / unhealthy foods?
- Why should we think carefully about what we eat?

Reading

- Draw pupils' attention to the fact that every day, in newspapers, magazines and on TV, there are articles on the latest ways to stay healthy and the best foods to eat. But which ones should we believe?
- Explain to pupils that they are going to read a newspaper article about healthy eating.
- The extract can be read to the class by the teacher, by individuals in the class or individually.

After reading

Use the panel prompts in the Pupil Book as the basis of a class discussion.

- What is the writer trying to persuade you to do?
  Eat healthy food instead of junk food.
- Name three healthy and three unhealthy foods.
  Unhealthy foods: any three of burger / chips / fizzy drink / pizza; healthy foods: any three of almonds / apples / grapes / fruit / vegetables.
- Who has written the article?
  The Association of Fruit and Vegetables for a Healthy Life.
- Explain the meaning of the bold words as they are used in the article:
  ***establishments:** businesses; **fare:** food; **contaminate:** poison / pollute; **benefit:** be an advantage; **E-number:** a number that represents a chemical added to food; **combats:** fights against.*
- Explain in your own words what the title of the article means.
  Answers that suggest that the food we put into our bodies affects how healthy we are.
- Why do you think the writer begins with a question?
  Answers that suggest that the writer is drawing in the reader who will read on in order to find the answer to the question.
- Why do you think the writer mentions 'scientists' several times?
  To make the article appear serious, as if it is based on scientific proof.
- Why do you think the writer uses the phrase 'no one but a complete idiot'?
  Answers suggest it is a strong phrase that 'persuades' you to agree with the article.

J Morgan
2, Oakfields Drive
Swinnerton
SW2 6ND

19th August, 2009

Stay Healthy Magazine
233 Marathon Way
Eastfields
London
NE5 9TE

Dear Sir or Madam,

I am writing to you having read with interest the article 'You Are What You Eat' in last month's issue.

I would like to state that I am all in favour of a healthy diet and eat my five portions of fruit and vegetables every day. I have no quarrel with 'what' is said in the article but for those lovers of junk food, it is hardly going to make them change their eating habits.

If you are going to persuade people to have a healthy diet, you have to stop throwing around words like 'scientist', 'miracle ingredient', and the mysterious sounding 'epicatechin'. Do you think we will be so impressed by words we do not understand that we will think what you say must be true?

The article refers on numerous occasions to 'scientists'. Who are these scientists? What experiments have they done? How many people have these miracle ingredients been tested on? What percentage have they worked on?

Newspapers and magazines are always full of the next 'wonder drug' and 'miracle cure'. Most of them never see the light of day again.

Stop treating your readers like morons. Give us some hard facts so we can judge how much research has been done and how effective it has been. It would also help if the writers of such articles did not have a vested interest in selling their products!

I will be scouring the shops to see if the wondrous apple fruit juice ever gets to the shelves!

Yours faithfully,

J Morgan

Understanding the letter

- Who is writing the letter?
- To whom are they writing?
- What is the letter about?
- The letter has seven paragraphs. Write briefly what each is about.
- Why does the writer end the letter with 'Yours faithfully'?

Looking at words

Explain the meaning of these words and phrases as they are used in the letter:

a issue　**b** portions　**c** impressed
d numerous　**e** wonder drug　**f** never see the light of day
g morons　**h** vested interest　**i** scouring

Exploring further

- What is the purpose of the first sentence of the letter?
- How do you know that the writer is 'in favour of a healthy diet'?
- Find evidence in the letter to show that the writer is not persuaded by the article *You Are What You Eat*.
  Look for:
  – things the letter writer says that the article included
  – things the letter writer says the article did not include.
- If the writer 'spoke' the last line of the letter, what do you think the tone of voice would be?

Extra

Discuss, draft and write a group letter to persuade your school to provide a choice of fruit and vegetables every day for lunch.

TEACH *continued ...*

- Do you think it is important to know who wrote the article or not? Explain your reasons.
  Answers that suggest it is important to know who wrote the article so as to decide how 'independent' the point of view is. 'The Association of Fruit and Vegetables for a Healthy Life' are likely to have a vested interest in people eating fruit and vegetables.
- Are you persuaded by this article? Why? Why not? *Individual answers.*

Plenary

- Pupils may have found the article persuasive, but discuss what would have made it more persuasive.
- You will have to 'lead' them to understand that there is not much foundation to the article. It is vague about the 'tests' done by the 'scientists'; there is no statistical evidence; its persuasiveness comes from its use of language rather than rigorous research.

TALK

Before reading

- Discuss why pupils think people write to newspapers and magazines.
- What do they write about?

Reading

- Ask pupils to recap on the article 'You are what you eat'.
- Explain they are now going to read a letter sent in by one reader of the article.
- The letter can be read to the class by the teacher, by individuals in the class or as a group.

Discussion group

In groups, pupils discuss the questions and make notes on their responses. Ensure pupils understand that they do not always have to agree.

Understanding the letter

- Who is writing the letter?
  J. Morgan.
- To whom are they writing?
  Stay Healthy Magazine.
- What is the letter about?
  The article 'You are what you eat'.
- The letter has seven paragraphs. Write briefly what each is about.
  ***1**: reason for writing; **2**: writer's views in general; **3**: the 'language' of the article – what is wrong with it; **4**: questions about the 'scientists'; **5**: wonder drugs and miracle cures; **6**: how to make the article more persuasive; **7**: conclusion showing that the writer is not convinced.*
- Why does the writer end the letter with 'Yours faithfully'?
  The correct ending for a letter where the writer does not know the name of the person he / she is writing to.

Looking at words

Explain the meaning of these words and phrases as they are used in the letter:

a ***issue:*** *magazine;* **b** ***portions:*** *amounts;* **c** ***impressed:*** *convinced / influenced;* **d** ***numerous:*** *many;* **e** ***wonder drug:*** *a medicine that can do marvellous things;* **f** ***never see the light of day:*** *never seen again;* **g** ***morons****: stupid people;* **h** ***vested interest:*** *personal interest in something happening;* **i** ***scouring:*** *searching thoroughly.*

Exploring further

- What is the purpose of the first sentence of the letter?
  Answers that suggest the opening sentence is designed to let the reader know immediately what the writer is writing about.
- How do you know that the writer is 'in favour of a healthy diet'?
  Answers based on evidence: 'I am all in favour of a healthy diet and eat my five portions of fruit and vegetables every day'.
- Find evidence in the letter to show that the writer is not persuaded by the article 'You are what you eat'. **ICT**
  Things the letter writer says the article includes – evidence such as: 'it is hardly going to make them change their eating habits' / 'stop throwing around words like...' / 'impressed by words we do not understand' / 'Stop treating your readers like morons'.
  Things the letter writer says the article does not include – evidence such as: 'Who are these scientists? What experiments have they done? How many people have these miracle ingredients been tested on? What percentage have they worked on?'
- If the writer 'spoke' the last line of the letter, what do you think the tone of voice would be?
  Answers that suggest the writer would be mocking / disbelieving / sarcastic.

Outlaw sunbeds

plea as cases of skin cancer soar

By **Lucy Johnston** and **Martyn Halle**

TANNING shops should be banned, says a leading skin charity, after revelations that children as young as eight have been using sunbeds.

Britain now has more skin cancer cases than Australia, an epidemic fuelled by an addiction to tanning.

Andrew Langford, chief executive of the Skin Care Campaign, says a whole generation of young people are raising their risk of developing skin cancer because of sunbeds.

Last week an all-party committee of MPs and peers demanded controls on tanning salons. Mr Langford wants them outlawed.

His call follows two recent events in Liverpool. One salon let an eight-year-old girl use a sunbed. Another allowed a pregnant mother to hold her three-year-old son while on a sunbed. Mr Langford said: "We were called by witnesses who couldn't believe their eyes. The sunbed industry is a disgrace.

"All evidence is that sunbeds are contributing to the skin cancer epidemic. The only way that ultraviolet light should be used is under close medical supervision to treat particular conditions." Members of the All Party Parliamentary Skin Group were shocked by new figures showing a 35 per cent rise in skin cancer over the past 10 years in Britain.

Every year 40,000 cases are diagnosed and there are 2,000 deaths.

Mark Goodfield, president of the British Association of Dermatologists, said: "Sunbeds are a major factor in the rise of skin cancer.

"Over exposure to ultraviolet light from sunbeds gives young people a 75 per cent chance of developing skin cancer as they grow older. We need to stop the under-18s going on sunbeds."

MPs want local authorities to ban sunbeds in leisure centres as this gives the false impression they are healthy.

Sunday Express, 16 November 2008

Understanding the article

1 What is the article trying to persuade people to do?
2 Who do the writers quote in the article?
3 Some people 'couldn't believe their eyes'. What had they witnessed?
4 What is the main idea of each paragraph in the article?

Understanding the words

5 Explain the meaning of these words and phrases as they are used in the article:

a revelations	**b** addiction	**c** outlawed
d contributing to	**e** medical supervision	**f** diagnosed

Exploring further

6 What effect do you think the writers want the headline to have?
7 Why do you think the writers quote Andrew Langford and Mark Goodfield?
8 What does Mr Langford mean when he says 'The sunbed industry is a disgrace'?
9 Why do you think the article uses figures such as '35 per cent rise in skin cancer' and '2,000 deaths'?
10 Explain in your own words why MPs want sunbeds banned in 'leisure centres'.

Extra

Write briefly to say why you are, or are not, persuaded by this article.

TALK *continued …*

Extra

ICT

- Discuss, draft and write a group letter to persuade your school to provide a choice of fruit and vegetables every day for lunch.

Ensure all members of the group contribute ideas. One pupil should take notes.

Plenary

- Read and discuss the letters for the 'Extra' activity.
- Choose the best one by a class vote.
- Ask individuals who voted for the winning letter to give their reasons.

WRITE

Before reading

- Discuss what pupils know about sunbeds.
- Why do people use them?
- Do pupils think they are a good idea? Why? Why not?
- Discuss the terms 'dermatology / dermatological'.

Reading

- Explain to pupils they are going to read a newspaper article with the headline 'Outlaw sunbeds plea as cases of skin cancer soar'.
- The extract can be read to the class by the teacher, by individuals in the class or individually.

Questions

Pupils answer the questions individually, drawing on their work in the previous class work (Teach) and group work (Talk).

Round-up

- Use pupils' answers to the 'Extra' activity as a basis for class discussion.
- Recap on what pupils have learned about persuasive writing, reinforcing:
  - use of persuasive language, e.g. 'soar' not 'go up', 'outlaw' not 'ban'
  - appeals to the reader, e.g. 'No one but a complete idiot'
  - research of facts to avoid vagueness.

Answer guidance

Understanding the article

1 Not to use sunbeds.

2 Andrew Langford – chief executive of the Skin Care Campaign; Mark Goodfield – president of the British Association of Dermatologists.

3 'A pregnant mother' holding 'her three-year-old son while on a sunbed'.

4 **para 1**: main reason why tanning shops should be banned; **para 2**: skin cancer cases in Britain; **para 3**: risk to young people; **para 4**: MPs' views; **para 5**: events in Liverpool; **para 6**: how ultraviolet light should be used; **para 7**: number of skin cancer cases every year; **para 8**: sunbeds and skin cancer; **para 9**: stop under 18s going on sunbeds; **para 10**: banning sunbeds in leisure centres.

Understanding the words

5 **a revelations**: surprising pieces of information; **b addiction**: a strong need to have / do something; **c outlawed**: made illegal; **d contributing to**: adding to; **e medical supervision**: when a doctor or nurse is present; **f diagnosed**: discovered.

Exploring further

6 Answers that suggest the headline is 'attention-grabbing', to draw the reader into reading the article. The words 'skin cancer' and 'soar' are meant to be shocking.

7 Answers that suggest they are 'experts' and what they have to say makes the case for outlawing sunbeds more persuasive.

8 Answers that suggest he means that the sunbed industry is irresponsible / dangerous / very bad.

9 Answers that suggest that the use of figures adds authority to an argument, that these figures are shocking and show the reader how serious the problem is.

10 Individual answers drawing on evidence of young children using sunbeds and the rise in cases of skin cancer.

Extra

Look for pupils to produce individual responses based on evidence in the text – they may find that the numbers and use of shocking individual stories make the article convincing; or they may question whether the numbers really say much.

A breakfast conversation

Roberta, Peter and Phyllis have been brought up in a comfortable and safe home in London in the early 20th century. Then one night, something happens, and afterwards their lives change dramatically.

When they came down to breakfast the next morning, Mother had already gone out.

'To London,' Ruth said, and left them to their breakfast.

'There's something awful the matter,' said Peter, breaking his egg. 'Ruth told me last night we should know soon enough.'

'Did you ask her?' said Roberta, with **scorn**.

'Yes, I did!' said Peter, angrily. 'If you could go to bed without caring whether Mother was worried or not, I couldn't. So there!'

'I don't think we ought to ask the servants things Mother doesn't tell us,' said Roberta.

'That's right, Miss Goody-goody,' said Peter, '**preach** away.'

'I'm not goody,' said Phyllis, 'but I think Bobbie's right this time.'

'Of course. She always is. In her own opinion,' said Peter.

'Oh, don't!' cried Roberta, putting down her eggspoon; 'don't let's be horrid to each other. I'm sure some **dire calamity** is happening. Don't let's make it worse!'

'Who began, I should like to know?' said Peter.

Roberta made an effort, and answered:–

'I did, I suppose, but–'

'Well, then,' said Peter, triumphantly. But before he went to school, he thumped his sister between the shoulders and told her to cheer up.

The children came home to one o'clock dinner, but Mother was not there. And she was not there at tea-time.

It was nearly seven o'clock before she came in, looking so ill and tired that the children felt they could not ask her any questions. She sank into an arm-chair. Phyllis took the long pins out of her hat, while Roberta took off her gloves, and Peter unfastened her walking-shoes and fetched her soft velvety slippers for her.

When she had had a cup of tea, and Roberta had put eau-de-Cologne on her poor head that ached, Mother said:–

'Now, my darlings, I want to tell you something. Those men last night did bring very bad news, and Father will be away for some time. I am very worried about it, and I want you to all help me, and not make things harder for me.'

'As if we would!' said Roberta, holding Mother's hand against her face.

'You can help me very much,' said Mother, 'by being good and happy and not quarrelling when I'm away' – Roberta and Peter exchanged **guilty** glances – 'for I shall be away a good deal.'

'We won't quarrel. Indeed we won't,' said everybody. And meant it, too.

'Then,' Mother went on, 'I want you not to ask me any questions about this trouble; and not to ask anybody else any questions.'

Peter **cringed** and shuffled his boots on the carpet.

'You'll promise this, too, won't you?' said Mother.

'I did ask Ruth,' said Peter, suddenly. 'I'm very sorry, but I did.'

'And what did she say?'

'She said I should know soon enough.'

'It isn't necessary for you to know anything about it,' said Mother; 'It's about business, and you never do understand business, do you?'

'No,' said Roberta. 'Is it something to do with Government?' For Father was a Government Officer.

'Yes,' said Mother. 'Now it's bed-time, my darlings. And don't you worry. It'll all come right in the end.'

'Then don't you worry either, Mother,' said Phyllis, 'and we'll all be as **good as gold**.'

Mother sighed and kissed them.

'We'll begin being good first thing to-morrow morning,' said Peter, as they went upstairs.

'Why not *now*?' said Roberta.

'There's nothing to be good about now, silly,' said Peter...

'I never wanted things to happen to make Mother unhappy,' said Roberta. 'Everything's perfectly horrid.'

Everything continued to be perfectly horrid for some weeks.

From *The Railway Children*, E. Nesbit

- Who are the characters in the story?
- Where is this part of the story set?
- What are the children talking about at breakfast?
- Where had Mother gone?
- When Mother returns, what does she:
  a tell the children?
  b ask them?
- Explain the meaning of the words and phrases in **bold** as they are used in the extract.
- What impression do you get of:
  - Phyllis?
  - Roberta?
  - Peter?
- What do you think 'happened' last night?
- Do you think the children ought to have been told what had happened to Father? Why? Why not?
- Do you think this is a modern or an old-fashioned story? Explain your reasons.

Extracts

The Railway Children E. Nesbitt
Little Women Louisa May Alcott
The Secret Garden Frances Hodgson Burnett

Planning

Older literature

Objectives

Renewed Primary Literacy Framework Year 5

3 *Group discussion and interaction*
- Plan and manage a group task over time using different levels of planning.

4 *Drama*
- Reflect on how working in role helps to explore issues.

5 *Engaging with and responding to texts*
- Recognise usefulness of techniques such as visualisation, prediction, empathy in exploring the meaning of texts.

7 *Understanding and interpreting texts*
- Use evidence from across a text to explain events.

Assessment focuses

AF2 Understand, describe, select or retrieve information, events or ideas from texts and use quotation and reference to text
  L3–L5 Increasingly use quotations, make inferences and deductions based on textual evidence.

AF7 Relate texts to social, cultural and historical traditions
  L3/L4 Make connections between texts, identifying common features; recognise and make simple comments on context
  L5 Recognise similarities and differences between texts, and explain how text context contributes to its meaning.

Scottish Curriculum for Excellence: Literacy

Listening and Talking

Finding and using information (third and fourth levels)
  Can make notes and organise these to develop thinking, explore issues and create new texts.

Reading

Finding and using information (third and fourth levels)
  Can make notes and organise them to develop thinking, retain and recall information, explore issues and create new texts.

TEACH

In this unit pupils will investigate older literature dating from 1906, 1868 and 1911 respectively. All the extracts concern children in difficult situations and show explicitly, or implicitly, their relationships with adults.

Before reading

- Discuss how pupils think the relationship between children and their parents has changed over the last 100 years. Are children more / less obedient? Are parents more / less strict?

Reading

- Explain to pupils they are going to read an extract from *The Railway Children*, a story that was written in 1906. The three children, Roberta, Peter and Phyllis, live happily until one day when their father is given bad news by a couple of men and leaves in a cab. Their mother doesn't explain why to the children. Read the extract, which begins at breakfast the next morning.
- The extract can be read to the class by the teacher, by individuals in the class or individually.

After reading

ICT

- Use the panel prompts in the Pupil Book as the basis of a class discussion.
- Who are the characters in the story?
  Ruth (the servant); Peter, Phyllis and Roberta (the children); Mother.
- Where is this part of the story set?
  In their home.
- What are the children talking about at breakfast?
  What happened the night before, a situation which Roberta thinks is a 'dire calamity'. Phyllis and Roberta agree that Peter shouldn't have asked Ruth about it.
- Where had Mother gone? *To London.*
- When Mother returns, what does she:
  a tell the children?
  'Those men last night did bring very bad news, and Father will be away for some time.'
  b ask them?
  '...I want you to help me and not make things harder for me...'; 'I want you not to ask me any questions about this trouble and not ask anybody else questions.'
- Explain the meanings of the words and phrases in bold as they are used in the extract:
  scorn: *a way of saying something that shows you do not approve;* ***preach:*** *tell people how to behave;* ***dire calamity:*** *a very serious event;* ***guilty:*** *ashamed;* ***cringed:*** *felt embarrassed;* ***good as gold****: behave very well.*
- What impression do you get of each of the children?
  Phyllis: the least talkative but says what she thinks; Roberta: likes to do the right thing / a bit bossy / admits she started an argument / doesn't like to quarrel / 'is a bit goody-goody' (according to Peter); Peter: headstrong, doesn't care about doing the 'right thing', feels bossed about by Roberta.
- What do you think 'happened' last night?
  Pupils should pick up the clue 'Those men last night did bring very bad news' and deduce that they were the reason Father went away.

Christmas presents

The story is set during the American Civil War in a small town in New England. Mr March is an army chaplain, and is at the front. The main characters are his four daughters and their mother.

'Christmas won't be Christmas without any presents,' grumbled Jo, lying on the rug.

'It's so dreadful to be poor!' sighed Meg, looking down at her old dress.

'I don't think it's fair for some girls to have lots of pretty things, and other girls nothing at all,' added little Amy with an injured sniff.

'We've got Father and Mother, and each other, anyhow,' said Beth contentedly, from her corner.

The four young faces on which the firelight shone brightened at the cheerful words, but darkened again as Jo said sadly:

'We haven't got Father, and shall not have him for a long time.' She didn't say 'perhaps never', but each silently added it, thinking of Father far away, where the fighting was.

Nobody spoke for a minute; then Meg said in an altered tone:

'You know the reason Mother proposed not having any presents this Christmas was because it's going to be a hard winter for everyone; and she thinks we ought not to spend money for pleasure, when our men are suffering so in the army. We can't do much, but we can make our little sacrifices, and ought to do it gladly. But I'm afraid I don't', and Meg shook her head, as she thought regretfully of all the pretty things she wanted.

'But I don't think the little we should spend would do any good. We've each got a dollar, and the army wouldn't be much helped by our giving that. I agree not to expect anything from Mother or you, but I do want to buy Undine and Sintram for myself; I've wanted it so long,' said Jo, who was a book-worm.

'I planned to spend mine in new music,' said Beth, with a little sigh, which no one heard but the hearth-brush and the kettle-holder.

'I shall get a nice box of Faber's drawing-pencils: I really need them,' said Amy decidedly.

'Mother didn't say anything about our money, and she won't wish us to give up everything. Let's each buy what we want, and have a little fun; I'm sure we grub hard enough to earn it,' cried Jo, examining the heels of her boots in a gentlemanly manner.

'I know *I* do, teaching those dreadful children nearly all day, when I'm longing to enjoy myself at home,' began Meg in a complaining tone again.

'You don't have half such a hard time as I do,' said Jo. 'How would you like to be shut up for hours with a nervous, fussy old lady, who keeps you trotting, is never satisfied, and worries you till you're ready to fly out of the window or box her ears?'

'It's naughty to fret, but I do think washing dishes and keeping things tidy is the worst work in the world. It makes me cross; and my hands get so stiff, I can't practise...'

'I don't believe any of you suffer as I do,' cried Amy; 'for you don't have to go to school with impertinent girls, who plague you if you don't know your lessons, and laugh at your dresses, and label your father if he isn't rich, and insult you when your nose isn't nice.'

From *Little Women*, Louisa May Alcott

Understanding the extract

- What are the names of the four daughters in the story?
- Who likes:
  - **a** drawing and goes to school?
  - **b** reading and looks after an old lady?
  - **c** music and does housework?
  - **d** pretty things and teaches children?
- Explain in your own words why there won't be any presents at Christmas.

Looking at words

Explain the meaning of these words as they are used in the extract:

a army chaplain **b** contentedly **c** proposed **d** sacrifices **e** regretfully
f decidedly **g** trotting **h** fret **i** impertinent **j** plague

Exploring further

- Why do you think each of the girls silently added 'perhaps never' when they talked about their father?
- How do you know the girls are not happy about not having presents?
- Each girl is going to use her money to buy herself a present. Is this what you would have done? Why? Why not?
- Which of the four girls do you think 'suffers' the most? Explain your reasons.

Extra

Imagine Mother comes into the room at this point in the story, and the girls explain to her what they have decided to do. How does Mother react? Role-play the scene.

TEACH *continued …*

- Do you think the children ought to have been told what had happened to Father? Why? Why not?
  Individual answers – they may worry more not knowing and be able to make their own judgement; the truth might be even more worrying.
- Do you think this is a modern or an old-fashioned story? Explain your reasons.
  It is old fashioned; evidence: the servant / children referring to their parents as 'Mother' and 'Father' / Mother wearing a hat with hat pins.

Plenary

- Discuss what pupils think might have happened to Father. Why did the two men visit him? Why did they take him away?
- How do pupils think they would have reacted in that situation?

TALK

Before reading

- Discuss the American Civil War with the pupils.
- It is unlikely that many pupils will have knowledge of this conflict but elicit / explain that a 'civil' war is when people of the same country fight each other. The North and the South of America fought over issues such as slavery.

Reading

- Explain to pupils they are going to read the beginning of *Little Women*, a story that was written in 1868.
- The extract can be read to the class by the teacher, by individuals in the class or as a group.

Discussion group

In groups, pupils discuss the questions and make notes on their responses. Ensure pupils understand that they do not always have to agree.

ICT

Understanding the extract

- What are the names of the four daughters in the story?
  Jo; Meg; Beth; Amy.
- Who likes drawing and goes to school?
  Amy
- Who likes reading and looks after an old lady?
  Jo
- Who likes music and does housework?
  Beth
- Who likes pretty things and teaches children?
  Meg
- Explain in your own words why there won't be any presents at Christmas.
  Answers based on evidence that the country is at war and Mother thinks that, as the men are suffering, people ought to make sacrifices and not spend money unnecessarily.

Looking at words

Explain the meaning of these words as they are used in the extract:

a ***army chaplain:*** *priest employed by the army;* **b** ***contentedly:*** *satisfied with life;* **c** ***proposed:*** *suggested;* **d** ***sacrifices:*** *things that are given up;* **e** ***regretfully:*** *sadly;* **f** ***decidedly:*** *firmly;* **g** ***trotting:*** *on the go;* **h** ***fret:*** *complain;* **i** ***impertinent:*** *rude;* **j** ***plague:*** *cause problems.*

Exploring further

- Why do you think each of the girls silently added 'perhaps never' when they talked about their father?
  Answers that suggest that as their Father is where the fighting is, he may die.
- How do you know the girls are not happy about not having presents?
  Answers based on evidence: Jo: 'Christmas won't be Christmas without any presents' / 'I don't think the little we should spend would do any good' / 'Let's each buy what we want and have a little fun';
  Amy: 'I don't think it's fair that some girls have lots of pretty things, and other girls nothing at all.';
  Meg: doesn't make the sacrifice of not having Christmas presents 'gladly'.
- Each girl is going to use her money to buy herself a present. Is this what you would have done? Why? Why not?
  Individual answers.
- Which of the four girls do you think 'suffers' the most? Explain your reasons.
  Individual answers.

The Secret Garden

Mary Lennox was born and lived in India. Then her mother and father die of cholera, and she is sent to England to live with her uncle, Mr Craven, in Misselthwaite Manor. It's a huge, unfriendly place and the only people Mary sees are the household servants. One night, she hears a 'Someone' crying and goes to investigate.

…she stood in the corridor and could hear the crying quite plainly, though it was not loud. It was on the other side of the wall at her left and a few yards farther on there was a door. She could see a glimmer of light coming from beneath it. The Someone was crying in that room, and it was quite a young Someone.

So she walked to the door and pushed it open, and there she was standing in the room!

It was a big room with ancient, handsome furniture in it. There was a low fire glowing faintly on the hearth and a night-light burning by the side of a carved four-posted bed hung with brocade, and on the bed was lying a boy, crying pitifully…

The boy had a sharp, delicate face, the colour of ivory and he seemed to have eyes too big for it. He had also a lot of hair which tumbled over his forehead in heavy locks and made his thin face seem smaller. He looked like a boy who had been ill, but he was crying more as if he were tired and cross than if he were in pain.

Mary stood near the door with her candle in her hand, holding her breath. Then she crept across the room, and as she drew nearer the light attracted the boy's attention and he turned his head on his pillow and stared at her, his grey eyes opening so wide that they seemed immense.

'Who are you?' he said at last in a half-frightened whisper. 'Are you a ghost?'

'No, I am not,' Mary answered, her own whisper sounding half-frightened. 'Are you one?'…

'No,' he replied after waiting a moment or so. 'I am Colin.'

'Who is Colin?' she faltered.

'I am Colin Craven. Who are you?'

'I am Mary Lennox. Mr Craven is my uncle.'

'He is my father,' said the boy.

'Your father!' gasped Mary. 'No one ever told me he had a boy! Why didn't they?'

'Come here,' he said, still keeping his strange eyes fixed on her with an anxious expression. She came close to the bed and he put out his hand and touched her.

'You are real, aren't you?' he said. 'I have such real dreams very often. You might be one of them.'

From *The Secret Garden*, Frances Hodgson Burnett

Understanding the extract

1 How did Mary know there was 'Someone' in the room?
2 When Mary went into the room, where did she see the boy?
3 Why did she think he was crying?
4 Why did Colin think that Mary might not be real?
5 What relation was Mary to Colin?

Understanding the words

6 Explain the meaning of these words as they are used in the extract:
   a glimmer **b** ancient **c** brocade
   d pitifully **e** ivory **f** immense

Exploring further

7 How do you think:
   a Mary felt when she saw Colin?
   b Colin felt when he saw Mary?
8 Would you say Colin's room was modern or old-fashioned? Explain your reasons.
9 Why do you think:
   a Mary was 'holding her breath' as she stood by the door?
   b Colin asked, 'Are you a ghost?' when he saw Mary?
10 Why do you think Colin had 'an anxious expression' on his face when he asked Mary to come over to him?

Extra

Imagine Colin and Mary go to see Mr Craven. They ask him why he had not told them about each other. Write Mr Craven's explanation.

TALK *continued ...*

Extra

ICT

- Imagine Mother comes into the room at this point in the story, and the girls explain to her what they have decided to do. How does Mother react? Role-play the scene.

  Remind the group about playscripts. Encourage them to set the scene, allocate roles, and to think carefully about their 'character' before writing the scene. They will need to discuss what kind of person Mother is. Make sure they understand the dilemma: the girls have decided upon a course of action which their mother may not approve of.

Plenary

- Discuss the situation the children find themselves in, in the first and second extracts, in terms of similarities and differences.
- If time permits, let groups act out their scenes.

WRITE

Before reading

- Discuss with the pupils that the British ruled in India until 1947.
- It is unlikely that many pupils will have knowledge of this but elicit / explain that when the British ruled India, many British people went out there to work and, consequently, many British children were born there.

Reading

- Explain to pupils they are going to read an extract from *The Secret Garden*, a story that was written in 1911.
- The extract can be read to the class by the teacher, by individuals in the class or individually.

Questions

Pupils answer the questions individually, drawing on their work in the previous class work (Teach) and group work (Talk).

Round-up

- Use pupils' answers to the 'Extra' activity as a basis for a class discussion.
- Ask pupils what they have learned about childhood over a hundred years ago.
- Would they rather be children now or then? Why?

Answer guidance

Understanding the extract

1 'She could see a glimmer of light' under the door; she could hear crying.
2 On the four-poster bed.
3 '...he was crying more as if he were tired and cross than if he were in pain.'
4 Colin has 'such real dreams' that he thinks Mary might be one of them.
5 Her cousin.

Understanding the words

6 a glimmer: faint; **b ancient**: very old; **c brocade**: rich fabric; **d pitifully**: unhappily; **e ivory**: pale yellow-white in colour; **f immense**: huge.

Exploring further

7 a Answers that suggest curious / a little frightened.
b Answers that suggest startled / a little frightened / couldn't believe his eyes.
8 Answers that suggest the room was old-fashioned, based on four-poster bed / brocade / fire.
9 a Answers that suggest she did not want to be noticed / did not want to startle the boy.
b Answers that suggest no one had told him about Mary and he seemed to spend so much time alone he couldn't believe she was real.
10 Answers that suggest Colin is anxious because he wants Mary to be real but is not sure she is.

Extra

Individual answers. Suggestions could include Colin being unwanted or born out of marriage and Mr Craven wanting to keep him a secret.

Unit 1

Trouble for Oliver!

Assessment

Name ____________________ Class ____________ Date ____________

		Type	AF	Mark
1	What is Oliver doing when he meets the Artful Dodger?	Literal	AF2	/1
2	Why does the Dodger think Oliver is running away?	Literal	AF2	/1
3	What does he give Oliver to eat?	Literal	AF3	/2
4	Besides food, what does Oliver need?	Literal	AF2	/1
5	Who is the Dodger going to take Oliver to meet?	Literal	AF3	/1
6	Explain the meaning of these words and phrases as they are used in the scene: **a** artful ____________ **b** urchin ____________ **c** magistrate ____________ **d** running from the law ____________ **e** grub ____________ **f** ravenously ____________ **g** slyly ____________ **h** earnestly ____________ **i** respectable ____________	Clarification	AF3	/9
7	What impression do you get of the Artful Dodger? Would he make a good friend for Oliver? Give evidence for your view.	Evaluation – empathy	AF6	/3
8	How does Oliver react to the Dodger?	Inference	AF3	/2
9	Why do you think Oliver is 'eating ravenously'?	Evaluation – empathy	AF6	/3
10	Why do you think the Dodger is 'looking around' all the time he is questioning Oliver?	Evaluation – historical context	AF7	/3

Total marks: /26

Do adverts persuade you?

Name ______________________ Class __________ Date ______________

		Type	AF	Mark
1	What is the purpose of the advertisement?	Summarising	AF3	/2
2	Who is the audience?	Inference – interpreting information	AF3	/2
3	Give two examples of persuasive words or phrases.	Analysis – language use	AF5	/2
4	Give two examples of information.	Analysis – text structure	AF3	/2
5	Explain the meaning of these words and phrases as they are used in the advertisement: **a** luxury ____________ **b** sun-drenched ____________ **c** world-class ____________ **d** spacious ____________ **e** sumptuous ____________ **f** limited ____________	Clarification	AF3	/6
6	Why do you think the advertisement begins with: **a** the cheapest price ____________ ____________ **b** a photograph of the cruise ship ____________	Analysis – text structure	AF4	/6
7	Look at the words 'luxury', 'elegant' and 'sumptuous'. Why do you think the writer uses these words?	Analysis – language use	AF5	/3
8	What does the writer mean when he says the islands are 'unspoilt'?	Analysis – language use	AF5	/2
9	Why do you think people would pay more for an 'outside twin cabin' than an 'inside twin cabin'?	Evaluation – social context	AF7	/3
10	Does the advertisement persuade you that this would be 'The Holiday Of Your Dreams'? Why? Why not?	Evaluation – criticism	AF6	/3

Total marks: /31

Understanding character

Name ____________________ Class __________ Date __________

		Type	AF	Mark
1	Who are the characters in the story?	Literal	AF2	/1
2	What are they doing?	Literal	AF2	/1
3	At first, how did they try to put out the fire?	Literal	AF2	/1
4	When Harry woke up, what did he think had happened?	Literal	AF2	/1
5	What was it that Harry knew they needed to put out the fire?	Literal	AF2	/1
6	Explain the meaning of these words and phrases as they are used in the extract. **a** instinctively ____________ **b** futilely ____________ **c** encirclement ____________ **d** deceived the eye ____________ **e** come to grips with ____________	Clarification	AF3	/5
7	Who is thinking more clearly when the fire starts: Graham or Wallace? Find evidence to support your view.	Evaluation – empathy	AF6	/3
8	Find evidence in the extract to show that Graham and Wallace panic as the fire spreads. Think about: what the author tells us; what the boys do; what the boys say.	Inference	AF3	/2
9	Graham says, 'We've got to get it out.' Harry says, 'We've got to get out of here.' How is each boy reacting to the situation? Explain in your own words why Graham and Harry are reacting so differently.	Evaluation – empathy	AF6	/6

Total marks: /21

Technology know-how

Name ______________________ Class ____________ Date ____________

		Type	AF	Mark
1	What are the instructions for?	Literal – finding information	AF2	/1
2	How many instructions are there?	Literal – finding information	AF2	/2
3	What key do you use to scroll down the MENU screen?	Literal – finding information	AF2	/1
4	What keys do you use to set the time?	Literal – finding information	AF2	/2
5	Explain the meaning of the words and phrases as they are used in the instructions: **a** hash key ____________ **b** menu ____________ **c** scroll down ____________	Clarification	AF3	/3
6	Why do you think the instructions are numbered?	Analysis – text structure	AF4	/3
7	Why do you think the instructions include diagrams?	Analysis – text structure	AF4	/3
8	Why do you think some words are in capitals?	Analysis – language use	AF5	/3
9	Think of at least three reasons why you might want to set an alarm on your mobile phone.	Evaluation – personal experience	AF6	/3
10	Do you think these instructions are easy to follow or not? Explain your reasons.	Evaluation – criticism	AF7	/3

Total marks: /24

Unit 5 Heroes and villains

Assessment

Name ______________________ Class ____________ Date ______________

		Type	AF	Mark
1	What did the Lin maiden do every morning?	Summarising	AF2	/2
2	What did the five dragon brothers do when they were angry?	Literal	AF2	/1
3	In her dream, how did the Lin maiden hold on to the ropes of her father's boat and her brothers' boats?	Literal	AF2	/1
4	What happened when her mother woke her up?	Literal	AF2	/1
5	When she realised her father was lost, what did the Lin maiden do?	Literal	AF2	/2
6	Explain the meaning of these words and phrases as they are used in the story: **a** launched ____________ **b** lash ____________ **c** collapse ____________ **d** seized ____________ **e** plunged ____________ **f** lantern ____________	Clarification	AF3	/6
7	What impression do you get of the Lin maiden?	Evaluation – opinion	AF6	/3
8	Why do you think she called out, 'Good wind and good weather' when the boats were launched?	Analysis – language use	AF5	/3
9	How do you think the dream made her feel?	Evaluation – empathy	AF6	/3
10	How do you think she and her mother felt as they waited 'through the afternoon and far into the evening'?	Evaluation – empathy	AF6	/3
11	Do you think the Lin maiden is the heroine of the story? Explain your reasons.	Evaluation – opinion	AF6	/3

Total marks: /28

Unit 6 Digging for the past

Name ______________________ Class ____________ Date ______________

		Type	AF	Mark
1	Where is the Valley of the Kings?	Literal – finding information	AF2	/1
2	How many tombs have been excavated? Name three things found buried with the pharaohs.	Literal – finding information	AF2	/2
3	How old was Tutankhamen when he became King?	Literal – finding information	AF2	/1
4	How do people think he died?	Literal – finding information	AF2	/1
5	The article has three paragraphs. Briefly say what each is about.	Summarising	AF2	/4
6	Explain the meaning of these words and phrases as they are used in the web page: **a** to date ____________ **b** excavated ____________ **c** plundered ____________ **d** after-life ____________ **e** sworn to secrecy ____________ **f** prompting ____________	Clarification	AF3	/6
7	What evidence is there that Tutankhamen's death was 'unexpected'?	Inference – deducing information	AF3	/2
8	Look at the sections at the top of the page. What would you expect to find if you clicked on: **a** Photos ____________ **b** Bookshop ____________ **c** Site Map ____________	Analysis – text structure	AF4	/6
9	Why are some of the words on the web page underlined?	Analysis – text structure	AF4	/3
10	Why do you think the page has advertisements for hotels and tours in Egypt?	Evaluation – social context	AF7	/3

Total marks: /29

Unit 7 Let me tell you a story

Assessment

Name ______________________ Class ____________ Date ____________

		Type	AF	Mark
1	What is the setting for the poem?	Literal	AF2	/1
2	Who are the characters in the poem?	Literal	AF2	/1
3	In what season does the poem take place?	Inference	AF3	/2
4	What living things does the poet see?	Literal	AF2	/1
5	What has the poet played on in the children's playground?	Literal	AF2	/1
6	Explain the meaning of these words and phrases as they are used in the poem: **a** announced ____________ **b** well on its way ____________ **c** scampered ____________ **d** flick ____________ **e** briefly ____________ **f** tug ____________	Clarification	AF3	/6
7	Explain in your own words why Dad thought it was a good idea to go to the park.	Inference – deducing information	AF3	/2
8	Look at these similes – 'soundless as snails', 'sharp as vinegar'. **a** What is each simile describing? ____________ ____________ **b** Do you think they are good descriptions? Why? Why not? ____________	Analysis – language use	AF5	/6
9	What does the poet mean when he: **a** says that the squirrel turned to 'grey stone'; ____________ ____________ **b** describes the slide as 'lonely'? ____________	Evaluation – author view point	AF6	/6
10	How do you think the poet felt about the trip to the park with his Dad? Explain your reasons.	Evaluation – empathy	AF6	/3

Total marks: /29

Far away from home

Name ______________________ Class ____________ Date ____________

		Type	AF	Mark
1	Where has the plane crashed?	Literal	AF2	/1
2	Which child is the oldest?	Inference	AF3	/2
3	Where has Peter been hurt?	Inference	AF3	/2
4	Give two examples of animals that would make noises during the night.	Literal	AF2	/1
5	Explain the meaning of these words and phrases as they are used in the extract: **a** gully ____________ **b** vastness ____________ **c** tension ____________ **d** ebb slowly ____________ **e** diminishing ____________ **f** recalcitrant ____________ **g** a far cry ____________ **h** meandered ____________	Clarification	AF3	/8
6	What impression do you get of: **a** Mary ____________ ____________ **b** Peter? ____________	Evaluation – opinion	AF6	/6
7	Why do you think Mary told Peter to 'suck' the barley sugar instead of biting it?	Evaluation – empathy	AF6	/3
8	Why do you think she put the other half of the barley sugar in her pocket?	Evaluation – empathy	AF6	/3
9	What do you think the author means when he says that the 'terrors' were 'all the greater for being unknown'?	Analysis – language use	AF5	/3
10	Why do you think Mary didn't sleep?	Evaluation – empathy	AF6	/3

Total marks: /32

Are you convinced?

Assessment

Name ______________________ Class __________ Date __________

		Type	AF	Mark
1	What is the article trying to persuade people to do?	Inference – interpreting information	AF3	/2
2	Who do the writers quote in the article?	Literal – finding information	AF2	/1
3	Some people 'couldn't believe their eyes'. What had they witnessed?	Literal – finding information	AF1	/1
4	What is the main idea of each paragraph in the article?	Literal – summarising	AF2	/1
5	Explain the meaning of these words and phrases as they are used in the article: **a** revelations ______ **b** addiction ______ **c** outlaw ______ **d** contributing to ______ **e** medical supervision ______ **f** diagnosed ______	Clarification	AF3	/6
6	What effect do you think the writers want the headline to have?	Analysis – language use	AF5	/3
7	Why do you think the writers quote Andrew Langford and Mark Goodfield?	Analysis – text structure	AF4	/3
8	What does Mr Langford mean when he says 'The sunbed industry is a disgrace'?	Analysis – language use	AF5	/3
9	Why do you think the article uses figures such as '35 per cent rise in skin cancer' and '2,000 deaths'?	Evaluation – author view point	AF6	/3
10	Explain in your own words why MPs want sunbeds banned in 'leisure centres'.	Inference – interpreting information	AF3	/2

Total marks: /25

Long, long ago

Name ______________________ Class ____________ Date ______________

		Type	AF	Mark
1	How did Mary know there was 'Someone' in the room?	Literal	AF2	/1
2	When Mary went into the room, where did she see the boy?	Literal	AF2	/2
3	Why did she think he was crying?	Literal	AF2	/1
4	Why did Colin think that Mary might not be real?	Literal	AF2	/1
5	What relation was Mary to Colin?	Inference	AF3	/2
6	Explain the meaning of these words as they are used in the extract: **a** glimmer ____________ **b** ancient ____________ **c** brocade ____________ **d** pitifully ____________ **e** ivory ____________ **f** immense ____________	Clarification	AF3	/6
7	How do you think: **a** Mary felt when she saw Colin? ____________ ____________ **b** Colin felt when he saw Mary? ____________	Evaluation – empathy	AF6	/6
8	Would you say Colin's room was modern or old-fashioned? Explain your reasons.	Evaluation – historical context	AF7	/3
9	Why do you think: **a** Mary was 'holding her breath' as she stood by the door? ____________ ____________ **b** Colin asked, 'Are you a ghost?' when he saw Mary? ____________	Evaluation – empathy	AF6	/6
10	Why do you think Colin had 'an anxious expression' on his face when he asked Mary to come over to him?	Evaluation – empathy	AF6	/3

Total marks: /31

G Using the Picture Snapshot Assessment

Donna Thomson

Reading and interpreting images provides a powerful and stimulating comprehension teaching and assessment tool for children of all ages and abilities. Pictures are full of inferred and hidden meaning and are a good starting point for comprehension instruction. This is because literal, inferential and evaluative visual clues are more immediate and easier to identify than text clues. Pictures can activate prior knowledge and experience in an instant. They prompt a range of emotions and personal reactions that absorb children and invite them to investigate and enquire further. The explicit teaching involved in the 'Snapshot Assessment' process helps children to develop essential thinking skills that can be transferred to other learning areas across the curriculum.

Picture Snapshot Assessment format

The 'Picture Snapshot Assessment' is an integral part of the Nelson Comprehension CD-ROMs. It provides an intriguing range of fiction and non-fiction stills and animated images with sound effects, accompanied by questions and answer guidance to test and assess a child's comprehension skills. The format is easy for pupils to use individually or in collaborative ability – or mixed-ability teams of two to five pupils. It is also designed for teachers to use as a smart board instruction model. We have related the pictures to the APP assessment focuses 2 to 7 and have grouped them in levels which approximate to National Curriculum reading levels 1 to 5.

Assessing strengths and weaknesses

Pupils' responses to the questions, and their own enquiry about 'Snapshot' picture narratives, offer teachers an excellent opportunity to assess their comprehension strengths and weaknesses. Assessment focus indicators that accompany each 'Snapshot' level provide teachers with a guide for assessment evidence gathered during each session. 'Snapshot' also assesses the comprehension skills of struggling decoders and pupils with language difficulties. The assessment process is effective because the absence of text (other than the title of a picture) allows the pupil the freedom to focus on comprehending, interpreting and choosing their own words to describe what is happening in a story, rather than on their struggle with decoding, which impedes their ability to understand the story in any depth.

Comprehension strategies

The 'Snapshot' activities are based on the Reciprocal Reading framework (Palicsar and Brown, 1986), a teacher-modelled scaffold that supports children's independent enquiry of fiction and non-fiction. Similarly, the 'Snapshots' are designed as an interactive process that helps children to read meaning within pictures, using the key comprehension strategies of summarising, predicting, questioning and clarifying. These key strategies draw on all assessment focuses except AF1. They encourage groups of the same or mixed ability pupils to delve deeply into picture narrative: extending their vocabulary, clarifying meaning and justifying viewpoints. It also helps them to develop the language of response and debate as they answer and generate their own literal, inferential and evaluative questions to monitor their understanding.

Using snapshots with small groups

While 'Snapshot' assessment is ideal for one-to-one assessment, it can also be used highly effectively with small groups of pupils. If the teams are unable to collaborate effectively, the groups will achieve little from the interactive activities. It can be very useful to define a specific role for each of the five to six pupils in the group (for example, a reader for the title and questions, a scribe, somebody to report back to the class, and someone to challenge their initial answers). The team members can take it in turns to experience these roles as they move through the different levels.

How 'Snapshot' works

Each picture still and animated sequence is specifically selected to assess pupils' ability to use key comprehension strategies to answer questions and generate their own questions. The titles of the images relate to the picture and sound clues that are linked to the picture narrative. The purpose of this is to encourage the reader to link the word clues to the images and sounds to explain what is happening and to predict narrative outcomes.

Hotspots

The clues in the picture narrative that tell the reader 'what is happening', 'what may have happened before' or 'what may happen next' are referred to in the series as 'hotspots'. Teachers and children are able to confirm the meaning of each clue by clicking directly on the hotspot to reveal the information. These clues range from literal 'who?', 'what?, 'where?' information, to inferred suggestions that require the reader to search for other clues to show how they have arrived at a conclusion, or why they think the characters are thinking or feeling in a certain way in the scene.

Screen 1 – section of whole image

The procedure on each level is progressive and extremely supportive. It begins with only part of the whole image shown on screen to encourage the reader to search for clues and link them to the title to predict what might be happening in the 'bigger picture' (rather like predicting contents from the cover of a book). The delving process also involves three literal questions that provide the basic information about the character(s), what they are doing and where they are; an evaluation question that asks them to consider what the characters might be feeling or thinking from their expression and body language; and a prediction question that asks them to calculate from the clues revealed what the story or 'whole scene' might be about.

Screen 1
Snapshot non-fiction level 5

Screen 2 – whole image

The next scene reveals the whole picture and asks the reader to look carefully at new clues. The initial questions are revisited to allow the reader to revise their previous view of what is happening as they answer again. Finally, there are two prediction questions that help them to consider what might have happened before and after the 'whole picture' scene.

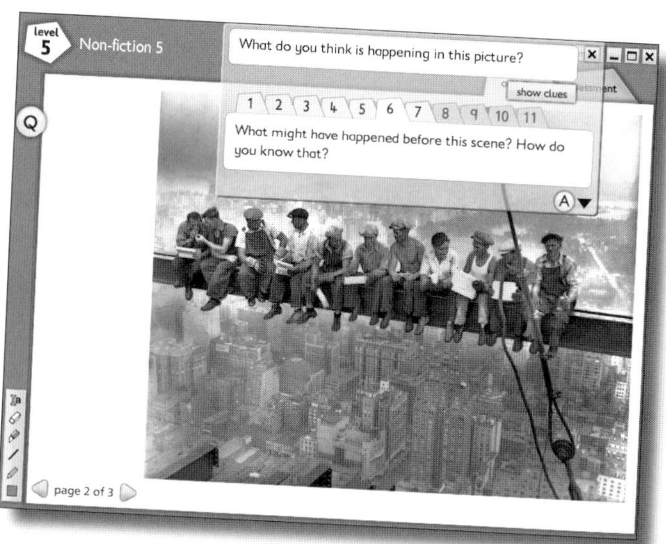

Screen 2
Snapshot non-fiction level 5

Assessment grid

The assessment at the end focuses on the accumulated answers to questions from screens 1 and 2, together with additional questions that ask the reader to generate their own query from a given answer to further assess their understanding and to measure their ability to ask literal, inference and evaluation questions. The final assessment score indicates possible areas for teacher intervention.

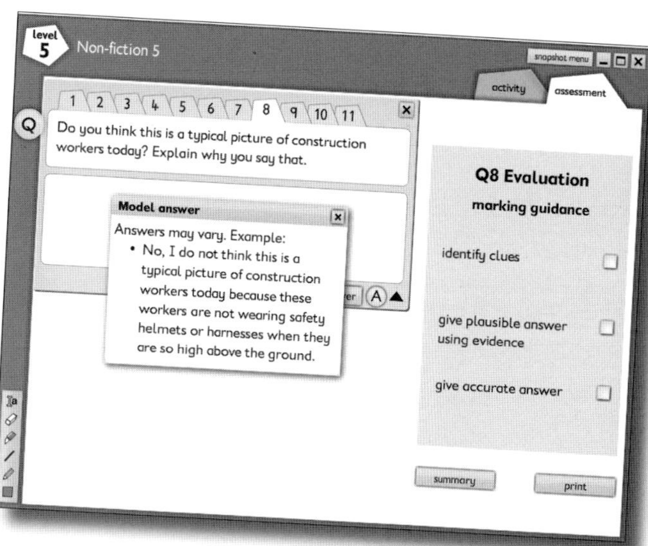

Each assessment question is supported by a model answer and marking guidance.

It is during the process of gathering and linking information to answer questions – and attempts at generating their own questions – that pupils' comprehension strengths and weaknesses are first exposed and the pupils themselves are able to identify areas of difficulty or lack of confidence. Throughout the process they are supported as they learn how to make links and connections between high and low levels of information.

'Snapshot' activities

The following levelled fiction and non-fiction 'snapshot' picture activities are designed to present a range of high- and low-level visual and sound clues that become more complex as the levels progress. Some are illustrations, others are black and white or colour photographs and many of them are animated. The purpose of these activities is to show children how to gather, clarify and organise information, how to identify the difference between literal and inferred meaning and how to make links and connections to solve problems. The animated clues have been included to draw the reader's eye to the hotspot information. The range of generic questions presented on each screen model a line of enquiry that the children soon learn and transfer to other areas of learning.

The first screen presents part of a whole picture. The reader first needs to read the title then look carefully at the picture for hotspot clues and listen for sound effects that suggest what may be happening in the narrative. The children's enquiry is guided by a series of questions that help them to gather information and make links of meaning between the clues on screens 1 and 2. The second screen shows the whole picture and includes further questions to support enquiry. These clues also provide confirmation of earlier predictions.

Snapshot: Level 1 Fiction – 'Halloween' (RA 5 yrs–6.5 yrs)

Visual type

Colour illustration with some animation and sound effects

Description

A pleasant looking woman is sitting in her cottage at the table pouring tea. It is night-time. Behind the woman we see children passing by, dressed in scary costumes. There are strange things happening in the room. There is loud banging at the door.

Screen information

Screen 1 – shows part of the whole picture

Hotspot clues: Black cat stirring pot, pouring green tea, children in ghost and skeleton outfits, lit pumpkin, moon in sky.

Sound clues: Bubbling cauldron, tea pouring, children's muffled laughter and chatter, loud banging on the door.

Screen 2 – the whole picture

Hotspot clues: Children in skeleton and monster costumes, witch's hat and cloak, Halloween date on calendar – 31st October, walking butter dish, sweeping broom, jar of sweets and jar of spiders.

Sound clues: Loud banging on door, children's voices shouting 'trick or treat', 'swish' sound of brush on floor occasionally.

What is happening?

The clues indicate that the children are 'trick-or-treating' because the title says it is Halloween. The children are dressed up in scary clothes and they are banging on the door and shouting 'trick-or-treat'. The clues also imply that the woman is a witch because of the hat and cloak on the door and strange goings-on in the house. The children are asked to consider what might happen if the witch opens the door to the children.

Snapshot: Level 1 Non-Fiction – 'Making Pizza' (RA 5 yrs–6.5 yrs)

Visual type

Colour photograph with some sound effects

Description

Four people working in a pizza factory.

Screen information

Screen 1 – shows part of the whole picture

Hotspot clues: Girl in white coat, plastic hat, mouth covered, man holding olives in gloved hand, machinery, pizza.

Sound clues (screens 1 and 2): Background radio music, sound of machinery and movement of production line, occasional cough, muffled voice counting 1 … 2 … 3 … 4!

Screen 2 – the whole picture

Hotspot clues: Pizza with four olives on, woman's hand reaching to put olives on bare pizza.

What is happening?

The clues indicate that the people are workers in a pizza factory because they are wearing protective clothing for hygiene reasons. They are all putting the same number of olives on pizzas in a line. There is the sound of machinery in the background and the title says 'Making Pizza'.

Snapshot: Level 2 Fiction – 'A Roundabout Ride' (RA 6.5 yrs–8.5 yrs)

Visual type

Colour illustration with some animations

Description

Outside a zoo by a funfair two zoo keepers are searching for something in the bushes. Children are running towards the roundabout ride. There is a tiger standing on the roundabout.

Screen information

Screen 1 – shows part of the whole picture

Hotspot clues: Sign pointing to zoo, zoo keeper with net, zoo keeper moving branch to peer into shrub, large paw prints, helter skelter ride.

Sound clues (screens 1 and 2): Fairground music, children laughing and squealing, tiger licking lips, smacking sound, girl's excited voice saying 'I want to go on the tiger ride!'

Screen 2 – the whole picture

Hotspot clues: Girl pointing at roundabout, end of tiger's tail twitching, tiger licking lips, girl on zebra ride looking worried, worried onlookers, excited children running up to roundabout.

What is happening?

The clues indicate that the two zoo keepers are looking for a tiger that has escaped from the zoo, because there are large paw prints leading to the roundabout where a tiger is standing. The tiger is pretending to be a ride on the roundabout either to avoid being caught by the zoo keepers, or because he is hungry and wants to trick a child into riding him so he can eat them – he is licking his lips. The reader is asked to consider what might happen next. Will the frightened onlookers tell the zoo keepers about the tiger before the children reach him?

Snapshot: Level 2 Non-Fiction – 'Dog Grooming' (RA 6.5 yrs–8.5 yrs)

Visual type

Colour Illustration with some sound effects

Description

The scene shows dogs being spruced up in a dog grooming parlour.

Screen information

Screen 1 – shows part of the whole picture

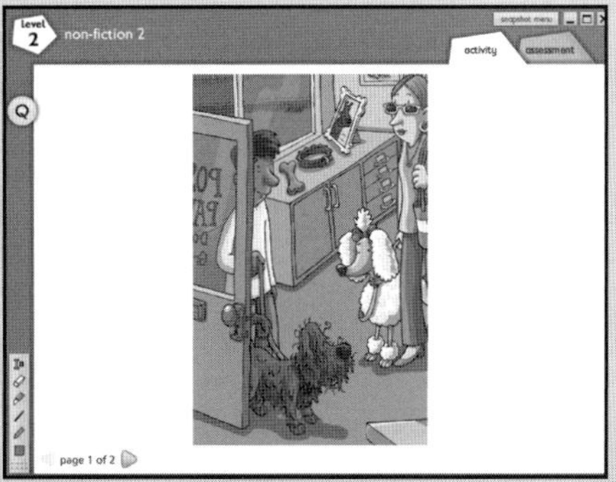

Hotspot clues: Perfect-looking poodle, dirty and scruffy-looking dog, 'Posh Paws' writing backwards on glass door, dog owner coming in – expression on his face (comparing the two dogs), dog owner going out – expression on her face (comparing the two dogs).

Sound clues (screens 1 and 2): Buzz of electric trimmer, sound of shower spray, voice saying 'Good dog', dog barking, dog whining.

Screen 2 – the whole picture

Hotspot clues: Two dogs ready to go home, electric trimmer, clipped fur (falling chunks of hair), girl's uniform ('Posh Paws' logo), man holding shower head, all dogs (except one in bath) have wagging tails.

What is happening?

The clues indicate that this is a place where dogs are washed and have their fur trimmed. The wagging tails tell us that most of them enjoy the experience, except the dog being showered. The clues further suggest that the dog owners take pride in the appearance of their dogs. The owner coming in looks embarrassed that his dog is so dirty compared to the perfect poodle going out.

Snapshot: Level 3 Fiction – 'All at Sea' (RA 8.5 yrs–10.5 yrs)

Visual type

Animated colour illustration with sound effects

Description

A boat has overturned in a choppy sea. A man who was hanging on in the water is now sitting on top of the boat calling for help. There is a man in a small boat nearby who is pulling another man out of the water. A person is watching from the shore.

Screen information

Screen 1 – shows part of the whole picture

Hotspot clues: overturned boat, hand clutching boat rope, top of head (turning to look at other boat), wave swell, floating apple, lunchbox, floating oar, life jacket, lightning/dark clouds, seagulls.

Sound clues: Seagulls crying, voice in panic to himself 'Oh no, it's getting closer', sound of wind/waves/sea.

Screen 2 – the whole picture

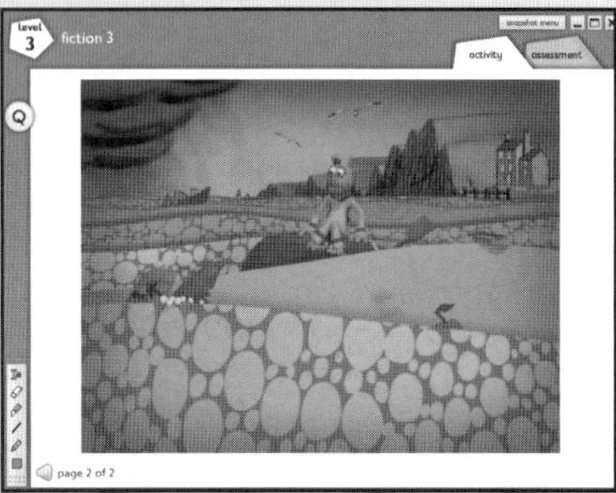

Hotspot clues: Frightened man jumps up onto boat, shark's fin circling boat, man pulling swimmer into boat, man swimming towards boat, person watching on shore.

Sound clues: Voice shouts out 'Help – over here!', sound of wind/waves/sea, seagulls crying, oar banging against boat.

What is happening?

The clues indicate that two men are out for the day and were just about to have lunch when their boat was overturned during a bad storm. Further clues suggest that a man in a small boat has come from the shore to rescue them, because someone is watching from the shore as he pulls one of the men into the boat. Another clue implies that the man who is calling for help may not be a strong swimmer, because unlike the other man, he has chosen not to swim to safety. The reader is asked to consider what might happen to him in the end.

Snapshot: Level 3 Non-Fiction – 'Fish for Dinner' (RA 8.5 yrs–10.5 yrs)

Visual type

Black and white photograph with sound effects

Description

Two men are in a moored boat and a dog is watching them from a jetty.

Screen information

Screen 1 – shows part of the whole picture

Hotspot clues: Boat tied to mooring post, heaped rocks, fishing rod, hatch cover, dog with collar looking at something going on.

Sound clues (screens 1 and 2): 'Swish' sound of line being cast, 'plop!' sound as hook and bait hit the water, men talking in French, sighing and chuckling, whining sound.

Screen 2 – the whole picture

Hotspot clues: Man sitting on left of boat, man sitting on chair smoking pipe, old-fashioned bamboo fishing rod, old-fashioned containers, man wearing French beret.

What is happening?

The sound clues indicate that the two men in the moored boat are French and out fishing for the day. The photograph is black and white, which suggests it is a scene from the past, and the men are smoking pipes and using old-fashioned equipment to fish with. The title implies that the men are not the only ones expecting fish for dinner – the dog is whining and looks like he is waiting for something as he watches them fishing.

Snapshot: Level 4 Fiction – 'Good Fit' (RA 10.5 yrs–11.5 yrs)

Visual type	**Description**
Colour illustrations with sound effects	There are four little men in the scene looking at a diagram, another is posing with a duck, two more are carrying a large roll of material, some are sewing and others are measuring. There is a giant pair of feet standing in the background.

Screen information

Screen 1 – shows part of the whole picture

Hotspot clues: Diagram of large man, spotted material, foreign language, pet duck on a lead, man puzzling over diagram and carefully observing something, large roll of spotted material.

Sound clues (screens 1 and 2): Snipping scissors, foreign muttering as background, other occasional voices ('mmmmh', sigh) thinking aloud, occasional quack.

Screen 2 – the whole picture

Hotspot clues: Pet duck on lead, big roll of spotted material, small man with megaphone, enormous shoe, hole in stocking, small men with needles working on material.

Screen 3 – the story conclusion

Image of giant being measured for clothes by little people.

What is happening?

The clues indicate that some little people are making new clothes for a giant because they are working from a clothes pattern designed for a large man. They are measuring, cutting and sewing big pieces of material to fit him. Also the story is entitled 'Good Fit'.

Snapshot: Level 4 Non-Fiction – 'World Championships 2008' (RA 10.5 yrs–11.5 yrs)

Visual type	**Description**
Colour photograph	Children and adults in a crowd watching a snail racing event.

Screen information

Screen 1 – shows part of the whole picture

Hotspot clues: Man shouting, expressions on faces of crowd – their age and gender, fence of flags.

Sound clues (screens 1 and 2): Male shouting 'Ready, steady, slow!' followed by background sound of small crowd talking, cheering and laughing occasionally.
In foreground, male and female voices shouting 'Come on, come on!'
Child's voice (laughing) 'That's the wrong way!'

Screen 2 – the whole picture

Hotspot clues: Outer red circle, inner red circle, snail moving inside circle, snail moving towards outer red line.

What is happening?

Clues indicate that people are racing snails in an important race because the photograph is entitled 'World Championships 2008' and there is a small crowd of spectators cheering on some snails that are moving across a table. Other clues imply that it is a race because all the snails are placed on a starting line in the centre of the tablecloth, and most of them are heading for the red line at the edge of the cloth, which suggests the finishing line of a race.

Snapshot: Level 5 Fiction – 'The Tea Picker' (RA 11.5 yrs–12.5 yrs)

Visual type

Colour illustration

Description

On a plantation set in an exotic landscape, the scene shows three women in Indian dress with large baskets on their backs. They are watching a well-dressed man sneering as he stands over a small girl who is weeping beside an overturned basket.

Screen information

Screen 1 – shows part of the whole picture

Hotspot clues: Foreign landscape, concerned looking woman in Indian dress, authoritative man looking at ground, crops, shadow.

Sound clues (screens 1 and 2): Tropical sounds, Indian voices (women murmuring concern), man making 'humph!' sneering sound, child sniffing (weeping).

Screen 2 – the whole picture

Hotspot clues: Women with baskets looking away and talking quietly together, tea leaves on the ground, tipped over basket, girl hanging head down, girl's foot curled awkwardly, man's hands on hips, man's facial expression.

What is happening?

Clues indicate that the scene is taking place on a tea plantation because the title refers to 'tea pickers', the women are carrying baskets and the little girl's overturned basket contains some leaves. Sound clues suggest that the girl is weeping because the overseer is sneering at her, either for dropping the large basket or because she has picked such a small amount. The reader is asked to consider what might happen next to the young girl.

Snapshot: Level 5 Non-Fiction – 'Making Manhattan' (RA 11.5 yrs–12.5 yrs)

Visual type

Black and white photograph with sound effects

Description

A line of workmen are sitting having a lunch break high above a city landscape.

Screen information

Screen 1 – shows part of the whole picture

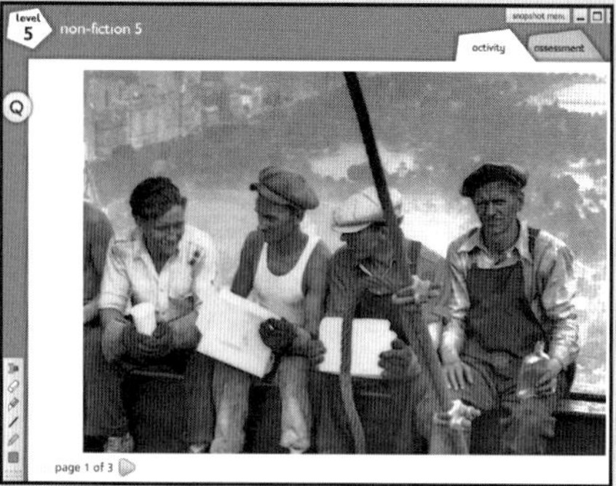

Hotspot clues: Cap, dungarees, lunch box, buildings in background, steel cable, vest.

Sound clues (screens 1 and 2): Sound of wind, male chatter and laughter.

Screen 2 – the whole picture

Hotspot clues: Two men lighting a cigarette (far left), work gloves (second on left), feet dangling, skyscrapers below.

What is happening?

The men are probably skyscraper construction workers because they are sitting on a steel girder high above a city of very tall buildings. Also the photograph is entitled 'Making Manhattan' which implies they are working on a Manhattan city building. The workers are all probably American because Manhattan is in the USA and there are also skyscrapers in America. Clues further imply that the photograph is a scene from the past because of the lack of safety equipment, the old-fashioned clothes the men are wearing, and the quality of the black and white photograph. Readers may wonder why the men are so relaxed sitting high above the ground when they are not protected from falling.

Analysing responses to questions

Gathering information, discussing and retelling is an essential part of the comprehension process. It is the first indicator of a reader's real engagement and basic understanding of the text or picture narrative. It shows how observant they are and what sort of reasoning skills they have. If they haven't grasped the main ideas when summarising the story information, the indications are that they are not looking closely enough; have poor language skills (vocabulary/phrasing) and sequencing ability; or have little personal or prior experience that links to the information in the picture. They may, as a consequence, give limited answers to the following questions about the picture narrative. The teacher may choose to give the individual or team a less demanding (lower level) picture to work from.

In the process of determining whether a student has answered a question correctly, the teacher needs to consider the following points.

- Does the reader's answer relate to the information in the title and picture?
- Is prior knowledge or experience being used to help explain a picture narrative?
- Does the reader understand the vocabulary used in the question?
- Does the reader have problems gathering literal or inferred information in response to questions?
- Does the reader have problems making links between clues to arrive at a conclusion?
- Is the reader engaged in the picture narrative?

Analysing responses to question types

Example: Level 4 'Good Fit' (Screen 2 picture)

Literal – explicit meaning – Who?, What?, Where? Right there! Information that is obvious and does not require interpretation.

Literal questions ask for answers that are found directly on the page. This simple form of questioning is essential when assessing whether a reader understands how to link key enquiry words in a question to basic key information within the text.

An example of a poor response to a literal question:

> Question: <u>*What*</u> are the characters <u>*doing*</u> with the large roll of *material*?
>
> Answer: The characters are making clothes.

Comment

The answer given here is an inferred response rather than an answer to a literal question. An inference question would need to include 'How do you know that?' to elicit this answer and evidence from the reader to support it.

The detail is clear in the picture. Although the reader has understood that many of the characters are *doing* something with material, they have not read the question carefully enough to identify who the question is directed at. The enquiry refers to the 'characters with the large roll of material' in the foreground of the picture and asks *what they are doing*.

> Correct answer: The *characters* are **carrying** the *large roll of material.*

Inference/Prediction – implied/hidden meaning. Information that is suggested within the narrative. The reader is required to think and search for clues that offer evidence to back up their response to questions.

Inference is not a straightforward question type. Although it allows for a variety of answers, all responses require evidence that relates to the picture or text information (in the title) and illustrator's/photographer's intention to support their answers. Answers that do not refer directly to the picture narrative are not acceptable – however reasonable and plausible.

An example of two poor responses to an inference question:

> Question: Are the *people* in the picture *making clothes* for a *giant*? How do you know that?
>
> Answer 1: Yes.
>
> Answer 2: Yes, because they have drawn a picture of him.

Comment

The first response does not fully answer the question because the second part of the question asks them to give evidence that shows how they know the answer is 'yes'.

The second response is incorrect because the reader has not considered the question closely enough. They have not accurately identified the clues in the question – *people, making clothes, giant* – and linked them to the inferred clues in the picture narrative – *little people, measuring and sewing material, clothes pattern, giant feet* – to provide an answer that is supported by clear evidence.

In addition, it is helpful for readers to know that if they use part of the question to answer with, it will guide their answers and help to keep them on the right track.

Correct answer: *Yes, the* ***people*** *in the picture are* ***making clothes*** *for a* ***giant****. I know this* because *there is a pair of* ***giant feet*** *in the picture and next to them much* ***smaller*** *people are* ***cutting*** *and* ***sewing large rolls of material*** *from a* ***clothes pattern*** *designed for a* ***very large man****.*

Evaluation – personal meaning. What you think characters may be feeling, doing or thinking from clues within the narrative and your own experience of life. Expressing an opinion based on information given.

Evaluation questions vary considerably according to the reader's own experience and prior knowledge. However, whatever their response, it must relate to the information given in the picture to be acceptable.

An example of two poor responses to an evaluation question:

Question: <u>*Do you think*</u> some of the <u>*characters*</u> are <u>*finding their task difficult*</u>? <u>*Why*</u> do you say that?

Answer 1: Yes.

Answer 2: No, because I think the design they are using looks easy to understand.

Comment

The first answer is incomplete because the person has not given a reason for their answer. The second response is inappropriate. The reader has not focused on all the key words in the question. Instead they have based their answer too much on personal opinion that is not supported by evidence from the picture. Although the reader has considered whether the '*task*' is '*difficult*', they have not linked this to the other key clue in the question that refers to the '*characters*' in the picture. Consequently, they have not looked for facial expressions and body language in the picture that suggest how the characters might be feeling or thinking about '*their task*'.

Appropriate answer: *Yes, I think some of the characters are finding their task difficult because* ***they are puzzling*** *over the clothes design and* ***looking unsure*** *about it.*

Clarification – understanding the meaning of vocabulary or a concept within the context of picture narrative. Defining the meaning of a word or concept from evidence available in a picture.

Readers of 'Snapshot' are asked to infer and define the meaning for words or ideas in the images by making links with clues in the picture narrative.

An example of a poor response to a clarification question:

> Question: There is a small man in the picture using a *megaphone*. Explain *what* he is using this *device* for.
>
> Answer: He is using a megaphone because he is making a long distance phone call.

Comment

The reader has answered the question incorrectly because although he has used prior knowledge to try to guess the meaning of the word, he has not referred to clues in the picture that suggest *what the device is* and *what it is being used for*. His answer does not make sense in the context of the picture.

> Correct answer: *The small man in the picture is using a megaphone to make his* ***tiny voice*** *louder so the tailors who are measuring the giant* ***high above*** *him* ***can hear what he is saying***.

Assessing levels – marking

Each comprehension level is a based on marks out of 20 that are represented as a percentage score at the end of the assessment, for example 2/20 = 10%; 12/20 = 60% and so on. The marks range from 1–3 points according to the question type. The marks for question types can be correlated with the QCA SATs marking system and are as follows:

- Literal: 1 point
- Inference: 2 points
- Prediction: 2 points
- Clarification: 2 points
- Evaluation: 3 points

The reader's total score represents a snapshot of their ability to gather information, summarise, predict, clarify and finally ask and answer literal, inferential and evaluative questions from pictures and titles. Ability within each level is measured to establish whether the reader or team need to drop down a level to help them to develop their comprehension skills further; need to remain at the same level to receive further instructional support; or are accomplished enough to move on to challenges on the next level. This can be used as evidence for a periodic assessment of the children's comprehension skills.

Comprehension ability within level

Easy/secure	score 70–100%	(move to next level)
Instructional/partial	score 40–65%	(remain at this level)
Hard/insecure	score 0–35%	(move down a level)

Notes